FANTASTIC FIGURES

SUSANNA OROYAN

Ideas & Techniques
Using the New Clays

C&T PUBLISHING

Copyright © 1994 Susanna Oroyan

Edited by Harold Nadel
Technical information edited by Florence Stone

Illustrations by Thomas Oroyan
Book design by Riba Taylor, Sebastopol, California

The copyrights on individual works are retained by the artists.

ISBN 0-914881-00-0

Library of Congress Cataloging-in-Publication Data

Oroyan, Susanna.
        Fantastic figures: ideas & techniques using the new clays /
Susanna Oroyan.
             p.   cm.
        ISBN 0-914881-00-0 (pbk.)
        1. Dollmaking.   2. Pottery craft.   3. Clay.   I. Title.
TT175.076   1994
738.8--dc20   94-4645
                                                       CIP

Published by C&T Publishing
P. O. Box 1456
Lafayette, California 94549

Printed in Hong Kong by Regent Publishing Services Ltd.
10 9 8 7 6 5 4 3

TABLE OF CONTENTS ———————————

CLOTHING

ACCESSORIES, DISPLAY, & FUN STUFF

MATERIALS

APPENDICES

WITH SPECIAL THANKS

to the dollmakers who so generously shared information and photographs for this book;

to Harold Nadel, my editor, who instigated and organized this book into printable form, and to the C&T Publishing team who recognized the growing interest in dollmaking and made this book a reality;

to Miriam Gourley, who brought us all together with "Dollmaker's Magic";

and, most especially, to my husband, Tom, for his love and continued support of my dollmaking and writing endeavors.

INTRODUCTION: DESIGNING YOUR DOLL

If you are really itching to get to the clay and start a doll, skip right on over to the next chapter and jump in, but do come back and catch up later!

Ordinarily, in a class situation, we would begin to work on our sculpture; as the day progressed, we would talk about the elements of "thinking" or "designing" that must be considered in making your own original dolls. Hands-on dollmaking doesn't have to be done in a logical order, but a book does. Thinking you want to make a doll comes before sculpting, so we will discuss that first. Most books will show you a step-by-step, how-to process that results in a specific finished project, like "How to Make the Little Green Elf." Since this book, however, deals with learning to make original sculpted dolls, not copies of mine, we need to talk about how to do *your own* original designing and planning—in short, how to turn your idea into a real doll.

At some point, you said, "I want to make dolls." (If you hadn't been thinking about dollmaking, you wouldn't be reading this book.) You have already been intrigued by the idea of making "little people," you have already been thinking you would like to create a character or a costume or a doll that could *do* something. You have probably even spent some time thinking about how to go about it. The minute you started this thinking, you were already making the doll in your mind. You were getting ideas and playing with design—probably the most important parts of dollmaking.

The primary difference between the beginner and the professional dollmaker is that the professional has had more experience with the planning. He has read a book or two, taken a class, probably made a few dolls; he has had some learning *experiences*. The beginner has just not had the opportunity to learn how to think a doll into reality. When I was nine years old, I had all sorts of dollmaking ideas. I knew exactly what I wanted my dolls to look like. Like most beginners, I had the skills: I could sew and cut and glue, but my young hands had just not done those things enough times in enough *different* ways to be able to pick the best way. I just did not have enough of the information that comes with experience. So, I quit.

Not too many people permanently retire from dollmaking at the age of nine and a half, and neither did I. I didn't try again until I was nineteen; although my skill experiences were better, I still hadn't really thought enough about the processes to create the desired results. However, the more I tried, the more I learned and the better I liked what I made. And, most important, the more I thought about what I was doing and learning, the better I got at figuring out the best ways of getting what I wanted. Nicola Tesla, the famous engineer, said that he usually built an engine in his head, and then, still in his imagination, without sketches or models, he started the engine and ran it for a week to see if it really would work. If he couldn't visualize any bugs in the design after a week, *then* he would draw the design on paper. So, let's begin to learn how to think about dollmaking.

In this country, original home studio art dollmaking evolved in the past forty years. We invented dollmaking by talking with each other, adapting any craft technique that might work, and by trial and error. From obscure chapters in children's craft books, from formal sculpture classes, and from self-study, little by little, our number of original doll artists grew. There was however, almost no means of communication beyond the small national organization of doll clubs until 1963, when Helen Bullard, Magge Head, Gertrude Florian, and Fawn Zeller got together with seven other dollmakers to found the National Institute of American Doll Artists (NIADA). We learned by invention, and so will you.

What was it we all invented? We invented something that most people would call a doll, but we also invented our own versions of "dollness." Each of us, each time we made a doll, re-invented the term. For some, it was the realization of a vision of exquisite female beauty; for some, a picture of the spontaneity of children at play; for others, a realistic photographic record of the man on the street or a historical figure; for still others, a manifestation from their imaginations and dreams. Every one of those visions, dreams, or snapshots was unique. Even if we each used exactly the same set of steps (which we didn't), the dolls we made were the result of those factors—education, interests, background, experience—that made up our individual personalities. So, we each evolved different steps and created different results.

This highly individual approach became very evident when I began to write the series of articles called "Dollmaker's Notebook" for the magazine *Doll Reader* in 1987. I thought I would be detailing certain technical processes but, very soon, the feedback from readers indicated that the parts they really preferred were those that gave a condensed version of the process, along with many ideas for them to see and think about. This "show me a bit" method of learning was again recently underscored by a dollmaker who called me about making armatures. I started to tell her that not much was available in print, and she said, "I don't need a set of lessons; I just want to see a picture of what one looks like."

This led me to think further about the theory of learning dollmaking. I realized that the step-by-step methods could not be totally successful; if the student for any reason missed a step, the whole process would fail to come out in the end. It became obvious that the student needed the tools to solve the problems, or the tools to teach himself another way around when faced with an obstacle. This meant teaching a whole lot about problem-solving and/or offering several methods of working with a material or process. Reasonably, even in the longest book, I could not cover *every* option. It looked like encouraging problem-solving would be a better approach.

I shut down the writing machine and went off to make dolls for two weeks. While I sculpted, painted, and stitched, I came up with this answer: In order to solve the problems we have in inventing our dollmaking, we have to look at what it is that we are doing. We are making dolls. What is a doll? What does it consist of? What skills are required?

If we think about it at all, we feel what we want to do is to make little people figures, sophisticated versions of antique or modern play dolls. Very few realize that what they really want to do is sculpture and applied design. Almost no one begins by addressing the idea that a doll, whether made for play or for pure aesthetics, is basically a work of art. In dealing with what to do with our hands, few of us had specifically addressed what to do with our heads—how to *think* a doll.

I began to realize that, if I wanted to write a book about dollmaking, I would have to consider teaching sculpture, applied design, research, the psychology of creativity and learning, some sociology (the human condition as interpreted in doll form), and a good deal about what happens when you do or don't do this or that with a particular medium—with a measure of self-confidence training thrown in for good measure. Quite a large order! So, I looked over what I had written so far. Had I done this? Was this what all the "talk" was? Yes, I thought it was, but a little more was needed.

Let's go back and examine the idea of a doll. No matter what its purpose or type, almost every doll is a representation of the human figure. The most interesting types to the dollmaker are usually those which represent some aspect of the human condition, real or imaginary. We make these little figures to express something we want to say to ourselves. This is sometimes therapy, sometimes to make an imaginary vision dimensional and tangible, and sometimes just to do it. Most dollmakers just need to see the idea finished up nicely: they don't need to sell the doll, they don't even need to have someone else see or like it. If there is one trait that distinguishes humans, it is probably that we will do something just because we had an idea and want to see if it works. Bringing imagination into reality is called *art*. However, not all art is *good* art.

Back to the idea of a doll. There are two basic types: the play doll into which the child puts messages or interpretations of the human condition during play, and the doll into which an artist puts an interpretation during its creation. Sometimes the artist's interpretation is as simple as "pretty little girl in party dress." If you pick up a doll magazine, you will note that the majority of humanoid dolls represent common social and cultural life. Almost like a photo album, they reflect some specific event in our lives, actual or fantasy: baby's first birthday, bride, woman shopping, famous historical person, Santa, fairy queen. Dollmakers want to make a three-dimensional memory piece, personal or cultural. Some execute their themes with photographic realism, while others choose abstract forms which make the viewer do a little personal thinking and projecting. Either way, the dollmaker must do something exceptionally good with the idea, or with the sculpture or costuming or pose, to make the piece special. This exceptional handling, which combines the principles of design and highly developed technical skills, makes the difference between ordinary interpretive art and good art.

Let's take the idea of baby's first birthday. Everyone can identify with the image of the dressed-up baby opening a gift box. Personally, the idea calls up an image of my son with cake smeared all over his face, his new suit, and the carpet. To make a doll that actually looked like that would require thought and consideration. First, would anyone want to look at and enjoy that image over several years? Second, how would you technically create the illusion of cake on the face? Paint it? Sculpt it? How would it look? Would a viewer understand what it was? So, "thinking a doll" requires making choices before starting to work.

Many dollmakers will scratch their heads and say, "But Santa is Santa. There are only so many ways you can do *that* figure." Not so. I can think of six different interpretations right now, not counting variations of costume, hair, and accessories. I can do that because I re-arrange the design and message components until a different image or interpretation emerges. So do other dollmakers. This is why we have so many interesting dolls. Thinking a doll requires you to open your mind to change. You need to look for things that you want to do, that you like to do, and that are different from what others have done.

Let's try it:

Typical Santa	New Santa
Old Man	_____
White beard	_____
Fat and jolly	_____
Red suit	_____
Black shiny boots	_____
Bag of toys	_____

Let's brainstorm a bit. Here are some of the ways your thinking could go:
- Santa could be a teen-age man, a child, an old woman, a young executive, an Afro-American woman.
- He could have a scraggly beard of natural mohair, no beard at all, an obviously false beard, a mask.
- Santa might be carrying diet food, be thin and gangling, be stuffed with a pillow. He might be tired or sad.
- Santa could wear a green brocade suit, or a business suit with fur trim.
- Maybe his cowboy boots are old and worn, he wears tennis shoes, he is barefoot, she wears silver evening pumps.
- Perhaps he carries a supermarket shopping bag, a cornucopia, filled with food—or guns.
- Maybe Santa is riding a surf board or a unicorn…

I have made at least a dozen Santas, mostly traditional, but one had a quilted bag, one was a businessman with a pillow around his waist getting into a Santa suit, and three were in their shirt sleeves doing pre-Christmas Santa tasks like reading the mail, writing the list, and making toys. This type of thinking is the truly necessary, original, and enjoyable part of dollmaking. It is essentially *design*—sorting through the maybes, the what-ifs, and the which-is-bests.

What we have done is called lateral thinking. Instead of doing the straightforward Santa thing, we went at the idea sideways from every angle. Each area we examined has potential subordinate variations. Let's continue. As concept, suppose we made a traditional Santa, just dropped down the chimney, harassed by the family dog? Shall we show the dog playing tug o' war with Santa's bag? Shall we show Santa flat on his back with the dog growling in his face? Shall we show Santa holding a bone behind his back?

What about Santa's face? I shall give you all the basic steps to get to the point where you will create a face the way you see it. Since I work with all those variations of Santa in my mind all the time, I am not capable of deciding at any given time exactly what Santa looks like to me. So, I sure can't tell you! What I can do is provide you with some tools to get, and hold, a visualization and to be able to create your own design plan from it.

Suppose you decide to pursue the idea of a traditional Santa playing tug o' war with the dog. Traditionally, Santa has a chubby face, a straight, medium-length Northern European nose, often with a little ball on the end, a full mouth "like a cherry," and little smile-crinkled blue eyes. When you add the final details in the top layer of flesh, you will create those features by adding or subtracting clay until it fits the picture in your mind. That is only part of your visualization. The other part has to do with expression. Santa probably didn't expect the dog to attack his bag. Is he surprised? Is he angry? You will need to detail the features to show the mobility of the face as it reflects the mood of the character. With a bearded figure this is a challenge. You can show the eyebrows curled down in a frown with forehead wrinkles, or you can show the eyebrows up and the eyes wide in surprise. What else is needed? Anything? Nothing?

Before you finish your sculpture, you must also anticipate two decisions: the kind of beard (sculpted or rooted or glued) and the pose. Will you need to sculpt hands and feet to accentuate the action? Learning to make a doll does not mean just sculpting the parts; it means questioning and decision-making at every step. Furthermore, it requires learning to be flexible at each step. Sometimes a problem can come up that requires a whole chain of ideas to change.

"But, hey, wait," you say. "You didn't tell me or show me how to sculpt that Santa head." No, I didn't. I can show you, maybe even take your hand in mine, place the tool exactly so, and move it exactly there. If I do that, then we have *my* sculpture. Even if you painstakingly follow me on video through over a thousand hand movements, you will have to repeat all of them twenty times over to pattern your hand and mind; even then, the patterning will be mine, not yours. If you practice the exercises on your own until your hands satisfy your eye, then you will have *your* sculpture. That's learning to sculpt.

I will show you how to construct a simple wire armature and cover it to make a basic human form. You must choose how to finish that body to suit your doll's character. Continuing with the idea of Santa Dogged: your traditional Santa will, of course, need to have a fully padded body. That padding, especially on the tummy, needs to be placed so that it will conform to the actual sag of a fat man's tummy, usually overhanging the belt. While you are making the body, you are thinking of the step behind and the step to come. The step behind was the scene you chose; the step ahead is the costume and final pose. Therefore, when you construct your wire body, you will want to bend it as close as you can to the way it will be in the final

pose. In our example, this would probably be bent over with the arms in front so he can pull on the bag. Oh, oh: problem time. If you do this pose with a fat tummy, how are you going to keep the figure from falling on his nose? Possible solutions? Weight his rear; plan for a base that will securely hold the feet, and balance the figure so that the weight is evenly distributed. Always bear in mind that your wire figure should stand in the pose by itself. Well-made dolls will stand by themselves, even in some very strange positions. It is a matter of playing with the construction and pose. Since I do not know what your doll will be, I can only show you the basic forms and tell you how to adjust them to fit your vision.

Always keep in mind that the idea of play is extremely important at any step of dollmaking. When you create a doll, you should not be in a hurry. You should experiment or play with any option that might come up. Play time always brings forth some good ideas and insights, and often some very good solutions.

Now we have progressed to the point where we have chosen a unique pose and interpretation, and we have underlined that choice by special sculptural details and by creating a body that will hold the pose and continue to say "chubby Santa" to the viewer. Next, we look at choices in the costuming that will further enhance that idea.

We decided to do the traditional red suit. First we will tend to look for red velvet. However, we have to check weight to make sure human-scale velvet will not be too large for the scale of this doll. If our figure is not tall, we might have to consider finding a lighter-weight fabric. We also require that the fabric be light enough to drape over the chubby tummy, to make nice wrinkles to enhance body motion if necessary. I could draw you a pattern for Santa pants and jacket, and you could make them exactly as I tell you, but that wouldn't work well because your figure might require adjustment in drape and shape to fit your chosen form. For good doll costuming, then, a dollmaker must be very familiar with pattern shapes for general types and then be aware that every single pattern has to be adjusted to fit the size, shape, and pose of the individual doll. It is a case of problem solving: how do I shape this material to make it look like what I see in my head? What material will shape this best?

Some of these problems are solved by knowing what is available, how it works, and where to get it. This means a dollmaker is constantly forced to keep up with advertising and magazine literature or keep an ear glued to the dollmakers' phone network. A cup of coffee and a good scan through magazines and catalogues will register tidbits like where wool felt or flesh-colored stockinette or hair straight from the goat can be purchased. Some things just aren't going to be available: you will have to create them yourself or find another solution. Don't assume that, because someone else has used a pattern or a material, it can be purchased. Don't ask where to buy the pattern. Ask yourself, instead, how to make the costume, or how to print the fabric to the scale required.

Finishing our Santa brings us to accessories and background. Here again, *you* think about how to make *your* idea just that much more individual and interesting. You have chosen a traditional look, but a tiny variation here and there couldn't hurt. How about changing the style of Santa's cap? How about adding some tiny decoration on his suit? Different buttons? Special belt buckle? *Traditional* is fine, but *ordinary* is boring. Add something!

Next we look at the bag. Choosing the material for the bag confronts the problem of showing the tugging between Santa and the dog. The solution will involve something that wrinkles, or having to create a pulled look. If your figures are well braced into the base, you can use a soft material. If you want leather, you will have to wet the material, mold folds and wrinkles, and figure out a way to glue or otherwise hold the wrinkles in place.

Now we come to the dog. I am really going to cheat on the dog problem. If I had decided to do this pose, I most likely would have had a dog already that I thought would work. If you do not have a dog, you will either have to find one or create a stuffed or sculpted dog in character and in scale with the Santa figure. The dog will have to show body tension, and he will have to be able to convey the clear idea to the viewer that he is, indeed, grabbing that bag in his teeth and pulling. I never said dollmaking was easy!

Just to tie up the whole piece, let's think about a base and background. Theoretically, our idea can stand as just two figures on a base covered to look like floor or rug. But wouldn't it be more fun if we had a fireplace, a chair, and a little table? Wouldn't these elements really fix the scene? Again, these are problems, and they are solved by examining and questioning the components. What is a fireplace? Bricks. How can I make bricks? Roll out Sculpey, cut bricks, and glue them together. Too hard. How about rolling out Paperclay and scoring it to look like bricks? Better. Shouldn't the mantle have something on it? How about a cat? What about a chair in the scene? No chair available is the right size. Have to make a chair. Where can we get a pattern for a chair? Check the catalogues. No pattern fits our image. Going to have to make a chair. Going to have to make our own patterns. What are the parts of our imaginary chair that we must put together? If you make the chair (or the table or the shoe or the hat), you as dollmaker actually will make something very close to the real-world item. Serious dollmakers know as much about costume as a fashion designer, as much about furniture as a cabinet maker, as much about hair styling as a beautician, and pretty much what a cobbler knows about shoes. Making the actual doll figure is often just a small part of creating the whole doll.

And so it goes. Learning to make a doll step by step is really learning to make a mental picture and then learning to take that picture apart, reduce it to shapes and materials, colors and textures, and then put it all back together so that it becomes a doll. At every stage we write our own instructions. We look at the image and we ask what it needs us to do to make it a doll, and if all parts work well together. Then we look at all the options for solving the problems. If we haven't learned or cannot research the option needed, we invent a solution that works with the materials or knowledge we do have. The purpose of a dollmaking book or class is to provide you with a short cut based on others' experiences, to aid you in researching some of the options for solving a doll problem you pose for yourself.

"But," you say, "I want to know how Mary Jane Dollmaker managed to get that particular effect." Apply the same principles to Mary Jane's work as you did to your own idea. Suppose Mary Jane's fabric looks like suede. How did she do that? You could ask her: dollmakers will usually tell you a trick or two. But if you can't, then ask yourself,

"How *could* she have done it?" Well, she could have painted on a suede-finish paint. She could have painted on something sticky and then shaken or blown fine powdery material on it. She might even have invented a flocking machine! Which of those could you do with what you have on hand or can find? Each artist takes from another's experiences and experiments, grows, and eventually finds his own direction. That's what makes dollmaking a "lively" art.

If, in these pages, you learned that a doll involves thinking, questioning, experimenting, and working to satisfy your mental pictures, then you have learned how to make a doll with any material. You could close the book right now and go make one. Or, you can read on to see if there might be a little more in the way of options and things to think about.

Milk and Cookies by Beth Cameron
18", Cernit and cloth over wire armature
Photo by John Wee

Traditional Santa by Kathy Gunson
33", Super Sculpey and cloth over wood armature. Photo by W. Donald Smith

Father Christmas by Rosemary Volpi
24", Super Sculpey, cloth over wire armature
Photo by Sam Schumacher

Father Christmas by Marilyn Radzat
36", Super Sculpey and cloth over wire armature. Photo by R. Sondgrath

It's Miller Time by Jodi and Richard Creager
15", Super Sculpey on wire armature
Photo by Richard Creager

Bobo Knickerbocker Van Beek Plays Santa by Susanna Oroyan
15", Super Sculpey on wire armature
Photo by W. Donald Smith

Santa by Betsey Baker
22", Paperclay and Super Sculpey, cloth over wire armature
Photo by Betsey Baker

Burgundy Santa by Bob and Anne Ross Anderson
34", Super Sculpey and cloth over wired wood
Photo by Anne Ross Anderson

St. Nicholas by E. J. Taylor
28", Super Sculpey head and Celluclay body
Photo by E. J. Taylor

SCULPTURE

In my sculpting classes, I spend as much time on concept and theory as on a "follow-me" set of steps. If you understand your goals, you can adjust the processes to suit your way of working. To begin, think of sculpting a piece, such as a head, as a process in which you begin with a space of air and you gradually fill that space with materials (armatures, clay, fabric) until an object you can call a doll occupies the space, much as a builder fills an empty lot with a house. The process is mostly additive: things are brought in and put together or added on; it is subtractive in that parts are trimmed and refined as needed. This process of sculpture is almost exactly the opposite of the woodcarver's method, where the artist takes away all the material that does not belong to his goal. In either approach, the main idea is *adjusting* materials as needed until they match your idea.

There are no really specific rules about how to adjust, but there are ways that seem to work better in general, and those that work better for some people. Certainly you can change the way things are usually done in order to reach a desired result. Although it is frightening for most beginners to realize that success or failure is up to you individually, if you can pick your way through the problems and find the solutions on your own, the feeling of achievement is far greater. "I figured it out myself" is always more satisfactory than "I copied exactly." There is nothing wrong with learning a skill by following a set of instructions; the problem with learning that way is that one mishap dooms the entire process.

Therefore, in the chapters that follow I am more concerned with telling you *why*—outlining the theory of dollmaking—than giving you a set of specific instructions. I am also most concerned with helping you to understand *how* things work in general and *which* things work best, in my experience. If you understand what you are after, and if you are familiar with several ways of getting there, then it will be easier for you to select the methods that will work best for *you*.

GETTING READY

When I first began to sculpt dolls, I picked up a hunk of Sculpey and the nearest tool-like object, a metal fingernail file, and just started to make a head. Then, I spent the next ten years refining my tools and workspace. You could, too, but I am going to give you a boost by outlining the basics that a working doll sculptor will find useful.

THE WORKSPACE

Because the pieces are usually rather small, you can work on doll sculpture just about anywhere—the corner of a dining table, television trays, adjustable hospital tables, and even airline fold-down trays. Dollmakers who work on full figures usually prefer a sculpting stand, which is available from an art supplier and adjusts for height much like a piano stool. This stand allows you to keep both hands free so you can work without tiring your arms. For working on separate parts or smaller figures, the best arrangement will be a desk or table top which is slightly lower than average—just high enough to clear your legs when you sit. The actual surface should be smooth and cleanable. You should have two movable sources of light: ideally, on one side a flexible-arm lamp with a magnifier, and on the other side a second flexible or gooseneck lamp. You will also find it helpful to have a turntable, either a sculptor's table-top model from an art supplier or the type used for kitchen storage. A 12" square of mirror glass or a hand mirror is also essential.

All sculpting clays get dirty. They attract pencil lead, printing ink, cigarette ash, dust, and sandwich crumbs. If you expose the material to dirty conditions, the debris will work into the clay. A dirt-marblized piece will have to be destroyed or heavily painted. Before you start work, wash your hands and clean your fingernails, and check that your sculpting surface is clear of all debris.

WORK SURFACE

Work on a smooth surface, such as counter-top plastic laminate, aluminum foil, or plate glass. Do be aware that some of the chemical components of the polymer clays can interact with some of the more brittle plastics, such as the plastic used for small storage boxes and drawer units. Sculpey, in particular, has been known to interact with certain flooring materials. When the polymer comes in contact with these plastics, it essentially melts into and bonds with them. If you are in doubt, test your surroundings or cover them while you work.

TOOLS

Anything you find comfortable in your hand or that will produce the effect you want is a sculpting tool! Most commercial sculpture tools (wood or metal) are made for working with ceramic clays and are usually unwieldy for working in doll scale. Some sculpture tools are made by or available from the polymer and paperclay manufacturers; however, they are primarily made for general craft work and

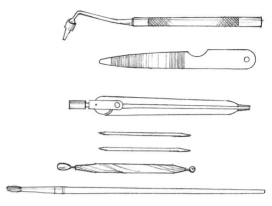

A selection of tools for sculpting

may not be able to achieve the detail you would like in dollmaking. Experiment with sculpture tools you find, and any of the following, until you find tools that fit your hand and habits best:

- thin metal fingernail file
- orange sticks, dowel sticks, toothpicks
- glass-head pins of varying sizes (use head to smooth small areas)
- dental tools (ask your dentist to save broken ones for you)
- water spray bottle (for smoothing surfaces)
- small embroidery scissors
- double-pointed drawing compass

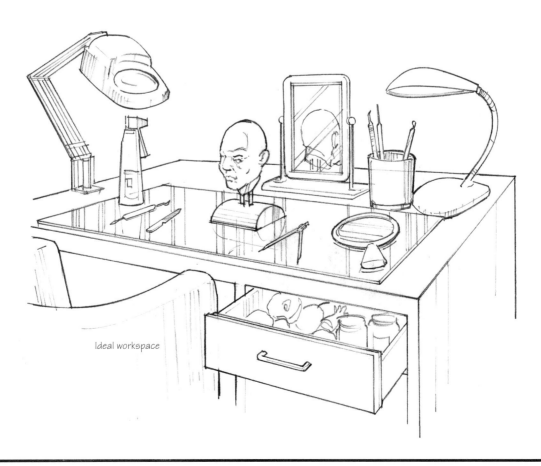

Ideal workspace

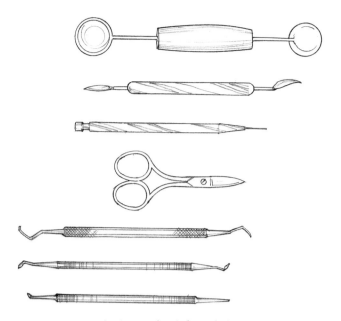

A selection of tools for sculpting

WORKING ARMATURES

Traditionally, in the art studio, a figure sculpture is done on a wire armature supported by a piece of pipe. The figure is sculpted in one piece, then the wires connecting it to the pipe support are cut and the clay figure is cut into body components. Molds are made from the parts, and the final figure is produced and assembled from parts cast from the molds. When this process is used in dollmaking, polymer clays can be used for the initial prototype sculpture and the result is usually a poured wax doll or a kiln-fired porcelain or china doll.

Ideally, everyone who sculpts a doll should sculpt the full figure, because that is the best and the easiest way to get good body proportioning. Since many dollmakers have chosen to make bodies of wire and fabric, they prefer to sculpt only the needed parts, checking proportions against sketches or charts rather than going to the trouble of sculpting a full figure. The type of working armature you choose will depend on the final doll type: prototype for mold-making, jointed figure, or a figure assembled on an armature.

In making dolls that will be assembled on wire armatures or cloth bodies, usually the head, hands, and legs are sculpted separately and hand-held while you work. For working on heads, it is easier to have a stand or temporary support, easily constructed from a few nails, a little wire, and wood scraps. Here are some variations you can try:

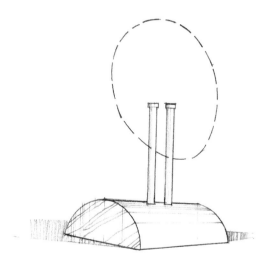

A simple head armature: two 3" nails set parallel in a piece of dowel

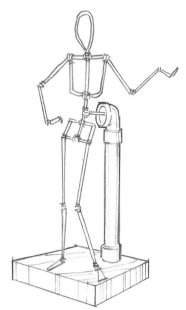

The pipe-supported, full-body wire armature

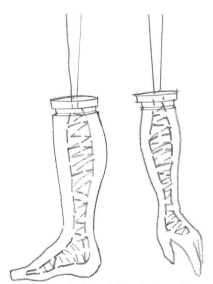

Armatures for limbs: foil crushed over wires

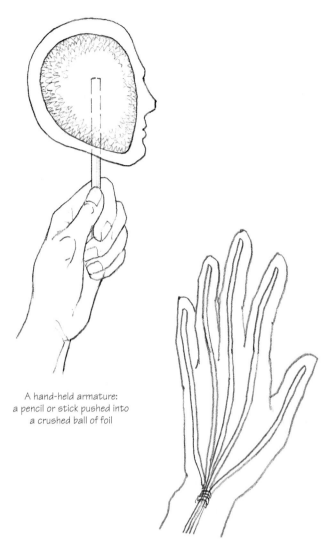

A hand-held armature: a pencil or stick pushed into a crushed ball of foil

A hand armature: wire loops for each finger are twisted together to form a bone structure

BEGINNING TO SCULPT

Planning Ahead

The fancy word for planning is "design." The first part of turning your idea into a successful reality is deciding what *type* of doll it will be and what *material* you will use. Those who have made or collected dolls will have some idea of the types and materials that exist, but let's review the options for the beginner.

Basic Doll Types

First is the play doll. This usually consists of a sculpted flange-neck head, sculpted hands and fore-arms, and sculpted feet and lower legs, all assembled on a stuffed cloth body. No supporting wires are used, and there are no joints.

Second is the flexible figure. This usually consists of the same sculpted parts as the play doll but, in this case, the parts are sculpted over wires connected to form a flexible skeleton. This is usually covered with cloth or batting, padded, and then covered with a fabric skin. The maker usually bends the skeleton into a fixed position during construction. These dolls are usually not meant to be moved after the figure is completed.

Third is the fully jointed, posable type. This is usually sculpted as a solid, complete figure, then cut apart, hollowed out, and jointed with springs or rubber bands so that it can be posed. This type gives you the advantage of having a doll that can be moved freely and that will sit or stand on its own without additional support.

Fourth is the solid figurine. This is usually sculpted over a pre-positioned wire armature and is permanently fixed. Makers will often choose this type when they wish to show a minimally costumed figure such as a fairy or a ballerina.

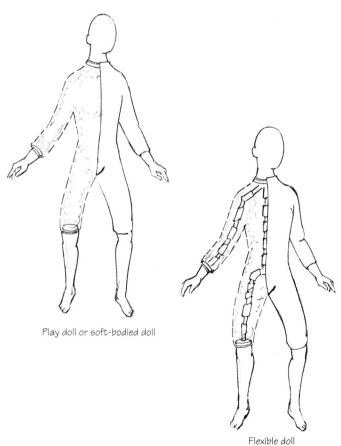

Play doll or soft-bodied doll

Flexible doll

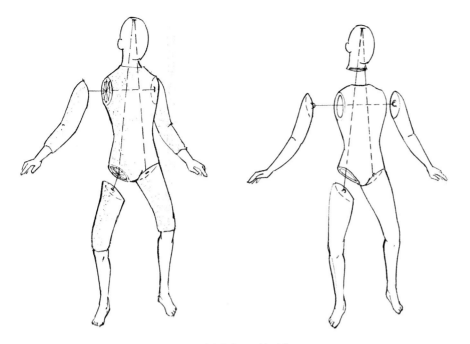

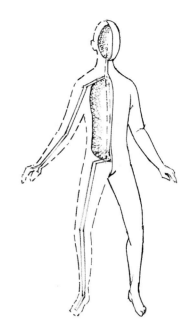

Jointed, posable dolls

Solid figurine

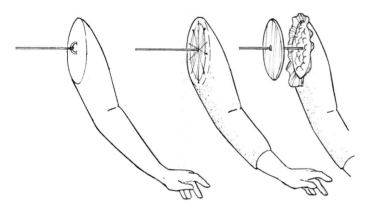

Detail of jointing on posable dolls

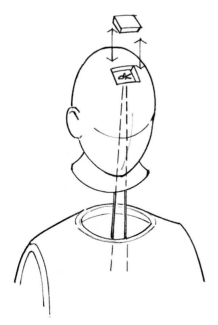

Detail of countersunk jointing on posable dolls

To make our categories more interesting, a creative maker will borrow a feature from another type, so that it is possible to make a play doll with a posable armature, or a flexible type with a solid torso, or any number of variations. The important point is that you consider how your doll is going to be assembled as you do the sculpture, so you can include the particular finishing processes needed for each particular type while the clay is soft.

Materials

For many years, dollmakers had limited choices. They could sculpt in soft oil-based or water-based clays, make plaster molds, cast in liquid ceramic slip, and fire the casting at high heat several times to make a porcelain or china doll; they could begin the same and cast a wax doll from the molds; they could make a cloth doll; or they could carve a wooden doll. These options were fairly frustrating, because ceramic forms involved time-consuming technical fussing and expensive equipment. It was very difficult to detail cloth realistically, and wood could not be sculpted by adding on. In recent years, with the arrival of well-made, widely available craft clay products, dollmaking options have multiplied. We can do just about anything we want!

Craft clays fall into two categories: air-drying (composition or ceramic clay) and oven-curing (polymer). The section on materials at the back of this book provides a brief description of the properties of most available types. In the United States, the most widely used air-drying clays are Creative Paperclay and Celluclay; the most widely used polymer clays are Sculpey, Super Sculpey, Sculpey III, Fimo, and Cernit. Since you can find these at your local craft supplier or through the suppliers listed in the back of the book, I will assume you are using these materials. If you are sculpting for the first time, Super Sculpey will be the easiest to learn and practice with. As you continue sculpting dolls, you should try all of the available products so that you can pick the ones best suited to your particular method of working and your objectives.

Attitude Adjustment

Most people are scared silly by the idea of actually sculpting. I know the feeling. I was terrified to try, and I made dolls for many years before I attempted sculpture. We tend to be so very "respectful" of the idea of sculpting the human form, because we are very conscious of what a complex piece of machinery it is. As for sculpting the human face, we become even more concerned because we place so much emphasis on the face as a mirror of personality and emotions. We seem to feel that if we don't get the sculpture "right," we are somehow not being respectful to ourselves and our fellow humans.

"Is this right?" is a question I hear from students time and again. Often, people who will take any collection of crazy materials and ideas to make a cloth doll will suddenly get very rule-bound and rigid when they try to sculpt. Sure, getting it right is important in sculpting but, in order to be successful and pleased with your work and, what is more important, to have *fun* with it, you need to have a large element of "so what" mixed in. In classes, I demonstrate this by throwing on the floor a piece of sculpture I have worked on most of the day. After the "Ohs!" have quieted down, I remind the class that it is, after all, just a piece of clay, and *I* am the one in control of it. You cannot expect to be perfect the first, second, or forty-second time you sculpt. I am here to tell you that you can still have problems after doing 300 sculpted dolls! So what if it doesn't work? Do another. So what happens if I try this or this? Remember, right now, this is for your own amusement: it is not a graded test, and it really won't make a difference to your life or livelihood if

you don't succeed immediately. Take your time, practice, experiment, and enjoy yourself. If you do, you will suddenly realize, "Hey, I'm sculpting!"

Using Your Head

Most of us expect how-to instructions to be diagrammatic or pictorial, so it might surprise you that the following lessons in sculpting are fairly wordy. When you are relaxed and well into working with clay, there comes a point when you seem to work automatically; your brain does not seem to be actively directing your hands. The act of moving clay around involves parts of the brain that deal with spatial relationships, and those are not the parts of the brain that "talk out loud," the parts involved in verbal thought. The chatty, thinking part of your brain needs to be involved, too. If you can teach it some of the theory and basic vocabulary of anatomy, you will find that it will act as a critic and teacher, reminding you at times when you need that sort of corrective input. When you can verbalize in simple terms associated with shape and position, the sculpting part of your brain will also hear and do the "right" things. For that reason, my instructions are diagrammed and accompanied by words and short key phrases. When you identify sculpting the eye, for instance, as the business of "putting a ball in a hole," you are reminding yourself in terms that all parts of the brain can work with. Try it; it works.

Using the Lessons

We are not going to approach sculpting in a straight-forward, step-by-step manner. Exercises, discussion, and explanations will make you take time out along the way and, in the long run, will help you get to trouble-free, happy results. I suggest that you read through a chapter and think about it once or twice before getting out the clay. When you feel ready to begin, do not commit yourself to doing just one doll. Start at least three heads. Stop and take time to do the exercises. Don't continue until you have tried the exercise once or twice—or as many times as it takes—to feel comfortable with the motions and ideas involved. Remember, it is just you and the clay, with no time-clock running. Some of the best sculptors will work up to a year, making many studies and experimental forms, before being satisfied enough to call a piece finished.

SCULPTING THE HEAD

BASIC HEAD SCULPTURE

You will need:

- Clay (beginners will probably find Super Sculpey easiest to handle)
- Tools (beginners will probably find a metal fingernail file most accessible and easiest to work with)
- Work surface
- Working armature
- Spray water bottle
- Aluminum kitchen foil
- Anatomy reference: dictionary, encyclopedia, medical or art book

The human head has a bony skull, a layer of muscles and tendons, and a layer of skin. When we sculpt a head, there are four very important things to keep in mind.

1. Because we are interested in character as expressed by the face, we tend to think of the face as *the* most important part of the head. The face is about one-quarter of the whole head. If the bone structure of the head is not correct, then the face cannot be successful.

2. Because we tend to look at and react to people's faces more than any other part of the body, we tend to spend a great deal of time concentrating on the face in sculpting: it gets bigger and bigger! Remember, the face is just one element of the expression of an individual's character. Body posture, body shape, and physical type are equally important.

3. The character we see expressed in the face is the result of the way the skin fits over the underlying muscles and bones. That means that the little details like character lines are just the very top layer, the finishing touch. If the muscles are not in the right place, the face cannot be successful. The more time you spend getting the skull and the muscles correct, the easier time you will have in making the face interesting and correct. Remember, the *last* thing you will do in your sculpture, *not* the first, will be the expression of individual character.

4. Another fact to remember in sculpting is that *you* are your best model. All the bones, muscles, and skin you will sculpt exist on you. Get familiar with your own body, its contours and its mechanics. Compare yourself to others around you. Most dollmakers, especially beginners, will automatically incorporate their own features or the features of those they are closest to.

Here, then, are the basic steps for creating the head of a mature adult:

Compress a 12" length of foil into the size of a golf ball. Cover it with a layer of clay about ⅜" thick. Add clay to form an egg shape. Take care to make surfaces even. Practice holding and turning the piece so that all areas are equal.

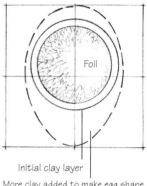

Initial clay layer
More clay added to make egg shape

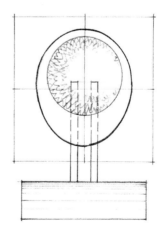 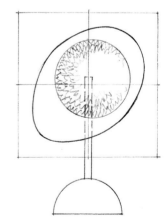

Front view of egg shape on armature (foreshortened)

Side view of egg shape showing foil ball inside

Spend a lot of time creating the most perfect egg you can. With your sculpting tool, score a line around the egg lengthwise. Hold the egg up to the light and look down the line, to check that the areas on each side of the line are equal. Teach yourself to compare equality of each side. Talk to yourself, describing what you see as you work: "Needs more here" or "Too flat there." If you do this, you will begin to realize that your brain and your eye really do see what needs to be done; you just have to listen and try to act on the messages from your senses. If necessary, add or subtract clay. Continue turning the egg and checking all sides for balance. Learning to see and correct imbalances will be important in your sculpting of the head. Check to see that each side is smooth and free of lumps. When you think your egg is as perfect as you can get it, make two or three more.

Place an egg shape on the working armature, as shown. Make sure supports are centered front to back and side to side. Keep the pointed end of the egg tilted down.

Stop, look at the diagram of the skull, and notice the similarities between the shapes of the skull and the egg. Notice also that the face and jaw hang *down*, forward and below the rounded back and top of the skull.

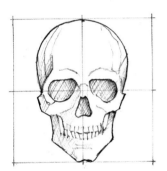
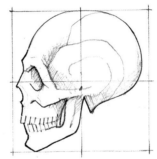

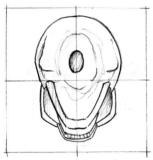

This is what the jaw looks like from beneath.

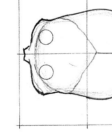

This is what the head looks like from above.

Notice that the eyes do not show: they are behind the eyebrow ridge. The facial area is rounded. All areas fall back from the center line of the face. Faces may appear to be flat when you look at them, but they are really rounded or peaked, much like the front of a boat.

Now take a few minutes to get acquainted with the shape of your own skull. Close your eyes and use both hands to outline the bony parts. *Talk* a description of what you feel: "The back of the skull starts just behind the ear lobe and goes in a fairly straight line across the back of the head." "The bone begins just in front of the ear lobe." Take both hands and feel where the bony part of your nose ends and the soft part begins. Feel the depression at the temple. Describe to yourself exactly *where* that depression is located. Is it below the center of the eye? Is it behind the end of your eyebrow? Feel the rim of the bone around your eye. Put your thumb on the lower rim of your eye socket and hold it there while feeling the thickness of the cheek bone with your fingers. Put your hand to your forehead and pull it away, holding the shape: your hand is following the curve of your forehead. Do the same with your mouth and notice the amount of curve: this corresponds to your jaws and teeth. Put your chin in the space between your thumb and forefinger. Pull your hand away and notice how sharp the angle is. When you study your face in this manner, you will begin to discover the parts that have to be underneath the clay skin in order to give the face its final shape and character; you are teaching yourself descriptive facial anatomy and creating the sound tape of instructions you need when sculpting.

Go over the parts again, still keeping your eyes closed, because it is important for you to *visualize mentally* what your fingers are telling you.

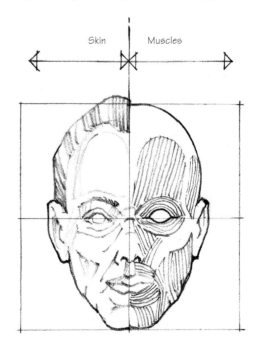

Skin   Muscles

Learning the shape of the skull

Take a moment to think about what you have learned. You have discovered that a head is a hard shell with holes in it: the eye sockets, the ear canals, the nose, and the space between your jaw and the cheek-sinus cavities where your teeth are located. Every human head you will ever sculpt will have the same bony shell and the same holes. Every time you sculpt a head, your own skull will be right there to help you remember where all the parts are. Don't leave your head behind when you sculpt!

Now, go back to the drawings of the skull. Review what you learned, by putting your finger on the drawings and tracing the shapes while you repeat your verbal instructions.

Continue to build your egg into a skull by adding a wedge of clay to the upper front, to create the forehead. If you pull your hair as flat as you can and look in a mirror, you will notice that almost one half of your head is above the eyes. Look at the drawing of the side view

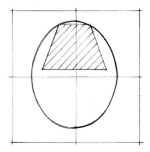

Front view (add forehead)

of the skull and notice that the forehead goes almost straight up from the eyebrows to the hairline. Be sure to allow your figure to have that brain space: don't cut him off above the eyebrows. Smooth the top of the egg until it looks nearly oval (slightly wider at the back than the front) when you look down on it.

Next, turn the egg so that you are looking at the side. With your tool, mark a line down the center, equally dividing the front from the back. Add a wedge at the lower back of the head to outline the lower edge of the skull and the back of the lower jaw. Again, notice that the jaw hangs down below the back of the skull. Now you have created all the bony parts of the skull. Smooth and blend. Take time to practice this skull-building process on the two other egg shapes you started.

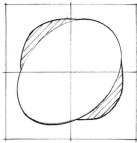

Side view (add back of skull)

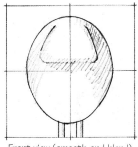

Front view (smooth and blend)

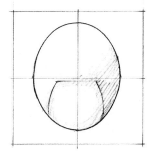

Side view (smooth and blend)

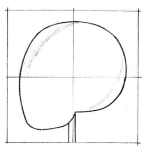

Top view (smooth and blend)

With the head facing you, slice off each side to flatten the egg shape.

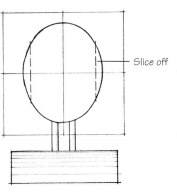

Front view

Side view

Holding your work so that you are looking at the side of the head, place the tip of your tool in the corner formed by the jaw and the skull, and press in slightly to form the ear canal. Place your thumb in that space on your own head and feel how the soft part of your ear just covers a space where the jaw

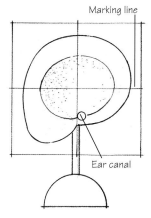

Marking line

Ear canal

and back of the skull come together. Notice how your ear lobe hangs outside and below this bony corner. Do the same for the opposite side of the head. Next, with the tip of your tool, draw a line dividing the side of the head into top and bottom halves. Do the same for the opposite side of the head.

Now turn the head so that it is facing you, and extend the line all the way across the front of the face. Draw a line down the center of the face, dividing it

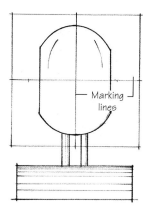

Marking lines

into two equal halves. Make sure both sides are equal: turn the head so that you can look at it from chin to top and from top to chin. Add or subtract clay, keeping the surface smooth, until both sides are equal.

Spend some time making the clay surfaces rounded and smooth with the palms of your hands. A spray from your water bottle will lubricate the surface and make it easier to work.

Looking straight at the face, draw a vertical line from top to bottom, exactly halfway between the side of the head and the center line. Repeat for the other half of the face. You now have three lines going down the face and one line going across. Put the point of your tool at the intersection of the horizontal line and the vertical side line: this is the center of the eye socket. Dig and turn the tool to make a deep hole for each eye socket. Do not be afraid to make it too big. If your own eye socket were empty, it would be big enough to hold half a ping-pong ball! Those holes should almost, but not quite, meet at the center line. Now, think jack o' lantern! Place the tip of your tool on the center line, just below the eye sockets, and twist it to make a wedge-shaped hole—the nasal cavity. In making the eye and nose holes, your tool probably lifted the clay around the edges of the holes. This lifting actually corresponds to the ridges of the bony structure of the skull.

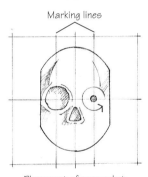

Marking lines

Placement of eye socket

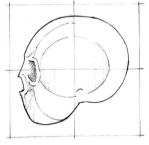

Side view

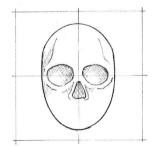

Placement of nasal cavity

You have now completed the first part of sculpting a human head: creating a skull with holes. Next you will fill those holes with the appropriate bits of soft tissue. But, before going on, take an important break.

1. Catch up by practicing the placement of holes, balancing the sides, and smoothing the surfaces on your other practice heads.

2. Put your practice heads aside for a moment. Do the following exercises several times on separate pieces of clay. When you feel you have mastered the concepts, then go ahead and apply them to your practice heads.

Eye Exercise

Notice that the eye goes into a hole in the head. Always remember that the eye is *a ball in a hole*. This eye-making exercise will help you understand the principle of the eye's anatomy.

a. Feel your own eye socket; run your fingers around the bone. Notice how big that hole is. The eye-socket hole goes from your nose to the side of your head and from the bottom of the "bag" to the eyebrow. Now feel how big your eye is. Your eyeball nearly fills that space. Note that only about one-sixth of your eyeball actually shows most of the time. Think about it!

b. Make a slab of clay about 3" x 3" x 1". With your knuckle, make a deep depression. Make a ball of clay about the size of your knuckle bone (about one-half the size of the hole) and drop it in the hole. This simulates the eye in the eye socket. Next, take a piece of clay and flatten it to the size of a quarter and about as thick. Cut it in half. Lay the flat pieces over the ball in the hole for the eyelids. Press the eyelid clay to the edges of the hole. This is the way your eye is constructed, and this is the way an eye is sculpted.

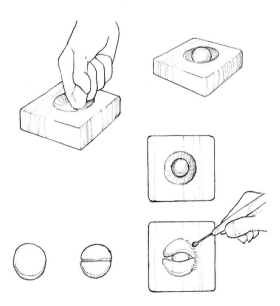

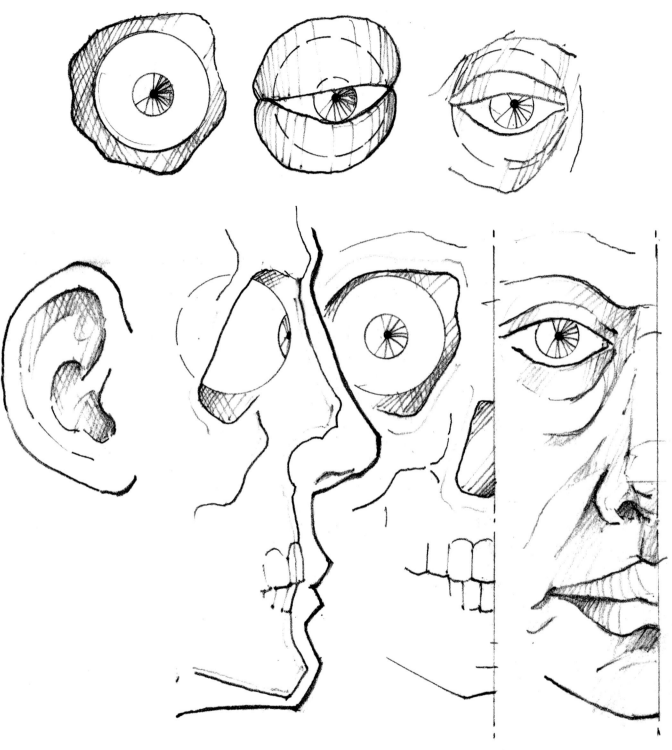

The anatomy of the eye

Mouth Exercise

Take a piece of clay and shape it into a rectangle about 5" x 3" x ½". With your tool, make a cut as shown in the diagram. Bend the piece over your fingers as if around teeth. As you bend, the cut will open, showing the inside edges. Those edges are the part of your skin that forms the lips. Any special shaping or extra flesh that makes a particular shape, such as a cupid's bow, is the result of extra flesh on those inside edges, forcing them into a larger curl. This is how a mouth is sculpted.

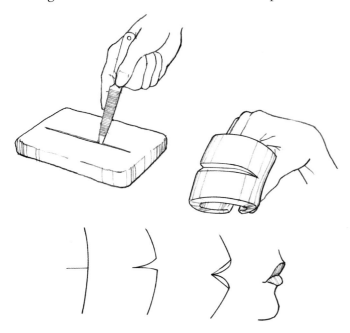

Nose Exercise

Return to a practice head and look at the nose hole. It is deep because the nasal cavity actually extends all the way up to your brain. As you put the point of a tool into the clay and turned it, the clay formed a ridge around the hole, very like the ridge that forms the bony bridge of a nose. Feel that bridge on your own nose. Notice where the bone ends and the soft part begins. The bridge is the part of your skull that determines the angle of your nose, its height and width. Take a piece of clay and roll it into an oblong ball; put the ball in the nose hole, pinching slightly as you push it in. This forms the soft part of your nose. If you wish, add a tiny ball at the end of the nose and blend it in. Add tiny balls at each side and blend for nostrils. To make the nostrils, push the tip of a flat-edged tool into the underside of the nose,

parallel to the nose, and turn. Remember, nostrils are not round holes: they are vertical, with wide variations depending on ethnic types.

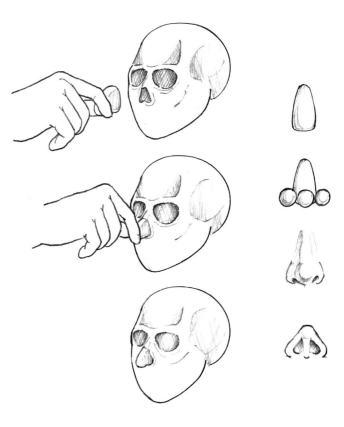

Ear Exercise

On a flat piece of clay about 3" long, make marks as shown. Those correspond to the marks on your practice skull which locate the ears. Make a ball of clay about the size of a large pea. Press it to the base clay with your fingertip so that a wedge is formed, the narrow edge blending to the base clay at the center line. Trim to a C. With the point of the tool, make an angled hole into the clay, as shown. This is your outer ear canal. Lift the tool and rock it up and down gently. The bit you lift on top of the tool forms the little part called the tragus. That is the part that sits forward of your ear canal and protects it. The part you press under your tool as you rock it forms the depression of your outer ear, the cup. Draw a groove as shown to make the upper curl of ear cartilage and cut away to define it. Add one tiny bit of clay to the bottom to form the ear lobe. With the tool, gently lift the ear wedge away from the base clay to form the outside shell. Feel the back of your own ear: notice that it is formed like a soup bowl with a wide, flat rim.

PUTTING IT ALL TOGETHER

Pick up one of your practice heads. Make an eyeball, then drop it into the hole so that the ball is below the edge of the hole and there is space around the ball. Remember, the upper edge of the eye hole is the brow bone, and the eye should not stick out beyond that brow; therefore, your eye socket hole must be deep as well as large. Cover the hole with pancakes of thin clay to form the eyelids. Define the eyelid and the edge of the eye socket by pressing the tool along the edge of the socket all the way around. Press so that the eyelid is slightly under the socket edge. Make an oblong ball and push it into the nose hole. Add extra balls for the tip of the nose and the nostrils. Make thin, triangular pancakes of clay and lay them over the lower face, as shown. Mark the mouth cut with the tool. With the tip of the tool, lift and roll back the clay to form the lips. Hold the head with your thumb and forefingers, and press gently to form the depression behind the eye at the temple. Once you have shaped both eyes and both temples, your head is roughed in.

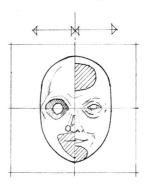

First-Stage Refinement

Holding the head with the face in profile, smooth and round the back of the head. Add more clay to the top of the head or forehead if necessary to achieve the form. Hold the tool perpendicular to the face, between the eyebrow area and the bottom of the eye socket. Make sure all the eye part is behind the line. Turn the head to face forward. Mark the line from the corner of the mouth to the nostril. Lay the tool flat along the line and press gently towards the back of the head to form the jowl line. Repeat for the other side. Formation of the jowl lines should result in definition of the teeth area, with a slight outward bow. Open the mouth cut and press open the edges with the side of the tool.

Groove

At this point, you should have the head shaped, jaw blended, eyes, nose, and mouth basic shapes in place.

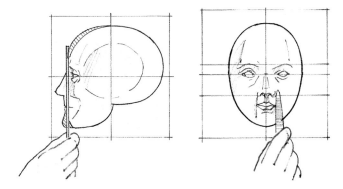

Second-Stage Refinement

With the head in profile, mark the line for ear placement as on the diagram. Be sure to hold the head so that the face is straight up and down when you make the marks; otherwise, the line will not fall right for correct placement. (Note that when you do hand-held sculpture, heads tend to float up into a skyward-looking position. From time to time, verify that your head is positioned on the working armature so that the face is parallel to the support and looking forward, not upward.) Repeat the ear procedure as you did in the exercise. Lay the tip of the tool against the head below the earlobe and make a depression which defines the back corner of the jaw. The back of the jaw will be just forward of the earlobe; verify the placement by checking where *your* bone ends.

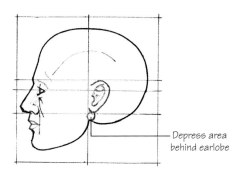

Depress area behind earlobe

Third-Stage Refinement

At this point, you are ready to detail some of the points where the bones and muscles make major impact on the facial sculpture. Basically, these areas have been sculpted as you created the skull.

They may have been lost as you added features. If so, you must re-define them. The points (such as bags under the eyes, or jowls) are present on all faces, but from person to person they vary in shape, depending on the individual's genetic blueprint. This means that any good sculpture will show them, but there will be no set rule for creating them. Now you are really beginning to do your own characterization!

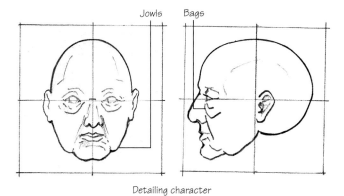

Jowls   Bags

Detailing character

Mouth

Unless you are making an exaggerated character, most upper jaws will be equal to or just slightly forward of the lower jaws and teeth. Thus, there will be a depression at each lower corner of the mouth. Indicate this depression with the tip of your tool, as shown. Because the muscles that open and close the mouth form a circle around the opening, a depression may form under the lower lip.

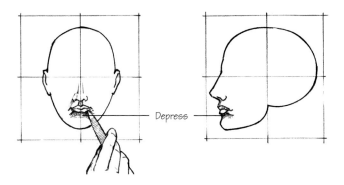

Depress

Nose

Because of the ridge of bone that forms the bridge of the nose, there is a slide of flesh off each side of the nose at the bridge. The bottom line of the slide is the jowl line, and the top is the upper cheek, just below the edge of the eye socket (the bottom of the "bag"). Depending on the individual, the fleshy part between the nostrils will create a slight depression on the upper lip. Remember that, on most humans, in a face-to-face situation, you do not see up the nose, but you will see the opening.

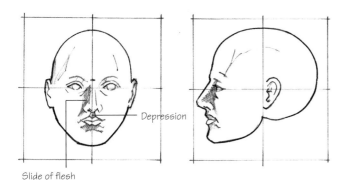

Slide of flesh

Eye

Depending on the height of the bridge of the nose, the eye will appear to be deep or shallow, heavily lidded or very thinly lidded. If the bridge is high, there will be a deep depression between the inside of the eyeball and the bridge of the nose. The area between the outside of the eyelid and the upper socket edge is usually a little more fleshy. If you are doing a character type or an older face, you might want to accentuate the lower edge of the eye socket, creating a bag.

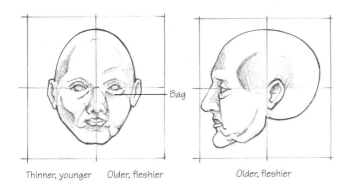

Thinner, younger   Older, fleshier   Older, fleshier

Cheeks

The cheek is a function of the way the skin falls from the lower edge of the eye socket and of the upper and lower teeth. People without back teeth will have sunken cheeks. Babies, young children, and heavier people will have very puffy cheeks. Some people will have round cheeks just because of their genetic composition.

Forehead

The upper bony ridge of the eye socket forms the overhang of the eyebrow line. When the skin goes over the forehead, a slight rounding is formed in the center of the forehead.

Temple

The temple area is a rather large depression in the skull behind the upper outside edge of the eye socket. This depression is almost, but not quite, filled with the cables of blood vessels, muscles, and tendons, so we see a slight depression.

Time to check for common errors and correct them:

- Eyeballs are too bulgy. Be sure they are behind the brow bone.
- Cheek bone is too high; there is no bag under the eye. Be sure you have suggested the lower half of the eye socket and its bag of flesh.
- Mouth and front of jaw are too flat. Remember, the mouth covers the *rounded* front of teeth. Depress the corners of the mouth to make it look like the lips naturally cover teeth.
- Nose is too wide. The widest part of the nose should not extend beyond the inside corners of the eyes.
- Ear is not correctly positioned. Tilt the head so that it is in profile looking straight ahead. Be sure the placement lines fall as shown. Remove any excess ear above or below the lines. With your tool, lift the whole ear and move it to the correct placement, if necessary.

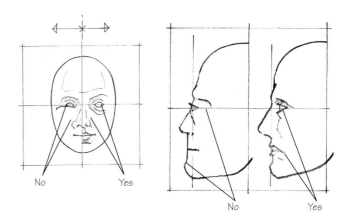

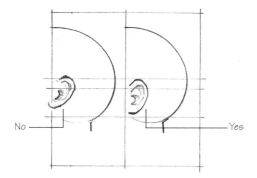

No ——— Yes

Stop!

Go back and make at least three more heads, following the directions closely from the beginning. (You can skip the exercises this time.) When you have practiced making the skull and bringing it to the roughed-in stage at least six times, you will be ready to finish your heads as specific character types.

TOOLS FOR REFINING THE SCULPTURE

•Water bottle: All materials will require smoothing as you sculpt. Paperclay will also need to be kept moist. Water does not affect polymer clay surfaces, but if it is applied to the surface when you are smoothing it, it acts as a lubricant for your fingers. The lumps will be easier to work away. However, spray *lightly*; too much water can cause bubbles. Over-watering will tend to make Paperclay surfaces slightly grainy. I rather like that effect but, if you prefer a very smooth finish, take care not to apply too much water. On the polymer clays, some artists like to use talcum powder or mineral oil to achieve the same lubricating effect. You might notice that, when water is used, the polymer surface takes on a slightly shiny, waxy look. With Super Sculpey, this almost always disappears during curing. Shiny marks made by hard metal tools will show on Fimo and Cernit, even after cooking.

•Acetone, nail-polish remover, mineral spirits, thinners: These materials will literally melt the surface of polymer clays, either cured or in the raw state. Although it is tempting to use them for short-cut cleaning, they are volatile and they do have harmful fumes. Avoid their use, or use with *extreme* caution.

•Mirror: In sculpture, we are dealing with a three-dimensional object. The difficulty we have to overcome is that we see only one area at a time, the plane exposed to our visual field, and we do not really think of that surface as being composed of ups and downs. This contouring of the surface has to be equal on both sides of the face. Faces might not actually *be* equal, but we see them that way; if we see an unequal representation of a face, it appears to be wrong. Thus, in doing good sculpture, the artist is forced to overcorrect.

To check the balance of features, forms, and plane lines, place the head so that it faces a mirror. Be sure the mirror and the head are parallel to each other. Look at the face in the mirror. If the face appears to be equal and balanced, then your sculpture is. Most of the time, you will find that the first mirror check will show that one side is sloping away at a sharper angle, or that the mouth is going up or down on one side where you thought it was straight, or that the eyes are not even. This unevenness is the result of the sculptor's dominant eye and hand taking over. Most right-handed people are right-eye dominant; when both hand and eye are doing the majority of the work, they will do it on the side they see best and are closest to. The mirror is used to trick the brain into seeing the neglected side prominently. Additionally, the mirror is used to give the dominant hand access to the difficult side. This is done by sculpting into the mirror: you look at the head as it appears in the mirror rather than as you face it when you sculpt. In that way, your dominant hand is working on your problem side.

•Double-pointed compass divider: This is used like calipers, to check the proportions; it is particularly useful for making sure features are equal in size and equally spaced on each side of the face. Set the compass so that the points fit into each eye corner. Without changing the setting, move it to the other eye and fit it in the same way. If the eyes are equal in width, the compass points will fit exactly. If not, you need to make adjustments. If you put the points of the compass in each inside corner of the eye, then the distance across these or between the eyes should be the same as one eye width. See the following chart for other applications of eye-width checking.

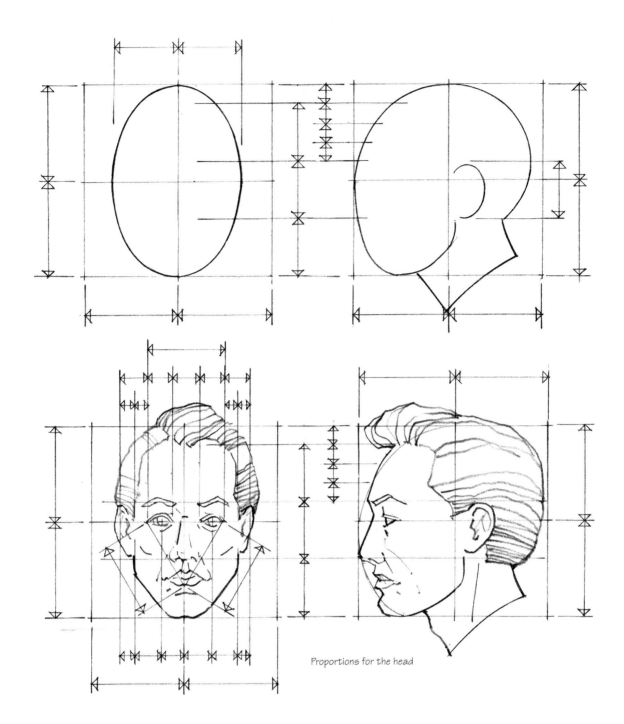

Proportions for the head

DISCOVERING AND DEFINING CHARACTER

Time for major decisions! At this point you have several heads that have all the correct human parts in the correct places. Now you can decide *who* they will be. Here are some key points to remember as you make your choices:

1. Skull shapes vary slightly. Some people have rounded skulls, some have very prominent bony ridges above the eyebrow, some have a very high,

bony nose bridge. Some have very short jaws that make them appear chinless or buck-toothed. These variations provide the underlying structure for the specific character we see in someone's face.

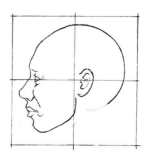

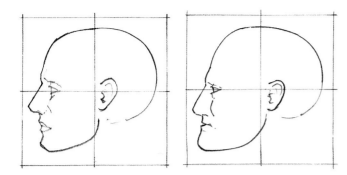

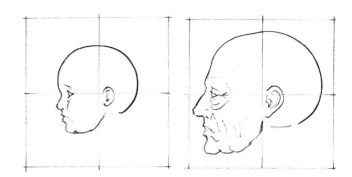

2. The part of the face that we usually identify closely with character is the skin as it falls over the muscles. The muscles might perform the same functions for each person, but they vary in structure from person to person. I have dimples. That means that, when I smile, you see an extra line in the flesh of my cheek. This is a depression caused by the particular way the muscles in my cheek are formed. A person who has a very prominent, fleshy lower lip has more muscle mass in that area. These characteristics are genetically linked which is, of course, why family members tend to share the same looks.

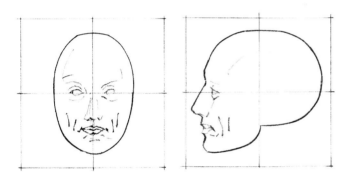

3. As you know, babies are chubby because their muscles are not yet well-defined and their bones have not matured to full size and shape. It might help you to think of character as a lifetime process of skin-stretching. As the baby grows, his bones and muscles grow, stretching the skin to the firm, smooth contours of youth and early maturity. As we grow older, the muscles lose their tone and the skin over them loosens. The loose skin falls in wrinkles along the line of the bones and muscles. It is very important for correct sculpture—realistic or exaggerated character—to make wrinkle lines follow the natural pull away from the underlying bones and muscles. It is also very important to remember that the fine surface wrinkles are the very last part of the wrinkling process. Those fine surface details also follow the underlying muscles.

For some different facial types, see the photographs on pages 32–33.

FINISHING THE HEAD

In order to complete your sculpted heads so they can be assembled into dolls, you will need to decide which type of neck-breast-torso attachment you want to use. See the doll types on pages 16–17 and the chapter "Constructing Bodies" which begins on page 65.

SCULPTING A NECK

1. Viewed from the front, the neck appears to be a straight column. The neck does *not* curve inward. (The action of your fingers in adding and smoothing clay will tend to make a depression in the neck: correct it.)

2. Viewed from the side, the neck angles forward. Feel the dent at the back of your neck. Feel how the neck curves inward and upwards from the nape to the base of the skull.

3. Major neck tendons are visible, running from the bottom of the ear to the V formed by the collar bones. These are very pronounced on a male. Male necks will also usually show a prominent Adam's apple.

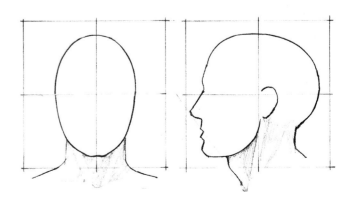

Thomas Trickster by Susanna Oroyan
Paperclay
Photo by W. Donald Smith

Beautiful Smile
by June Lunsford Goodnow
Super Sculpey
Photo by Brian Schul

Three Angels by Sandra Babin
Paperclay
Photo by Sandra Babin

Is It Me? by Nancy Walters
Paperclay
Photo by Nancy Walters

Achille by E. J. Taylor
Paperclay
Photo by E. J. Taylor

Little Mermaid
by Elisabeth Flueler-Tomamichel
Super Sculpey
Photo by Christophe Flueler

Court Jester by Jane Covington
Super Sculpey
Photo by Bruce Bailey

Baby by Susanna Oroyan
Paperclay
Photo by W. Donald Smith

Sohailla by Patricia Ryan Brooks
Super Sculpey
Photo by Patricia Ryan Brooks

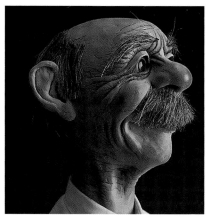

Abner by Bill Nelson
Super Sculpey
Photo by Tim Gabbert

Mending Lady by Scott R. Gray
Paperclay
Photo by Scott R. Gray

Eve by Ellen Poitras
Super Sculpey
Photo by Nancy Walters

Daydreamer by Carol Trobe
Cernit
Photo by Terrence McGarrigle

Polka Dot Hat by Katherine Paiva
Super Sculpey
Photo by W. Donald Smith

Starring in the Follies by Van Craig
Papier mâché
Photo by M.J. Magri

Ashia by Judith Klawitter
Super Sculpey
Photo by Mark Bryant

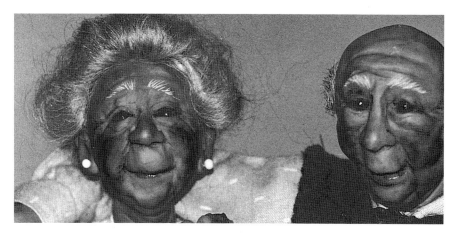

Courting Couple by Annie Wahl
Super Sculpey
Photo by Annie Wahl

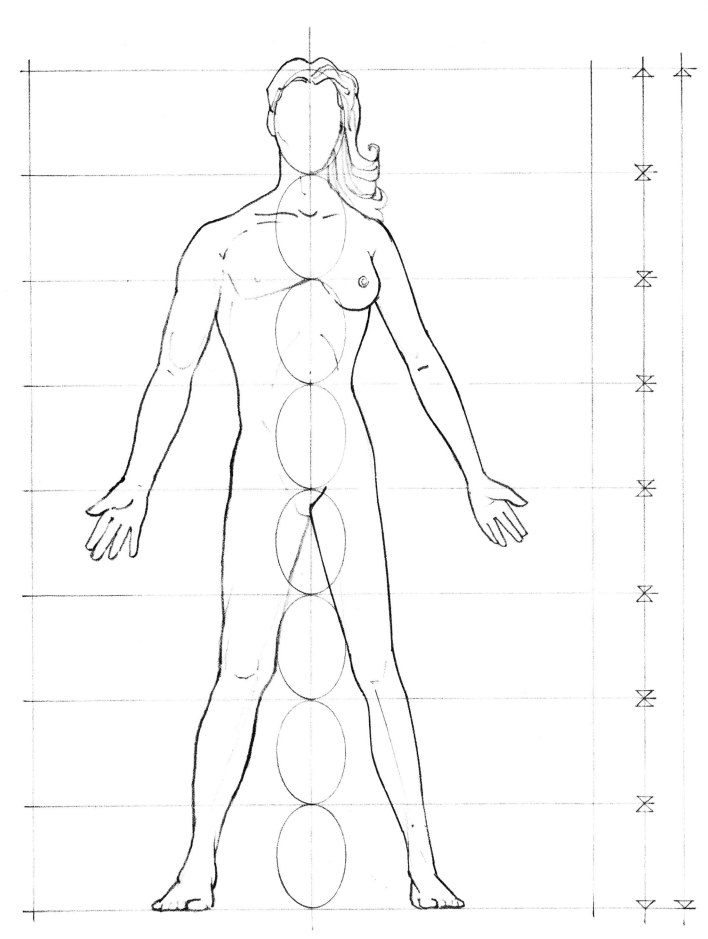

Proportions for the body
Based on a doll proportion of 8 heads = typical body

SCULPTING THE BODY

HANDS

Three different types of hands are used in doll sculpture: human-like but abstracted; "play doll," human-like in proportion but smooth and static; character or realistic, part of the total expression of the character.

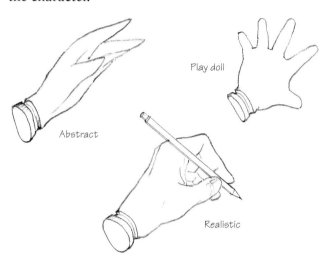

In most cases, you will have already finished the head when you sculpt the hands. To make hands proportional to the head, there are two quick rules: from the bottom of the palm to the end of the middle finger will be as long as from the chin to just above the eyebrows; the nose will be about as wide as the index finger.

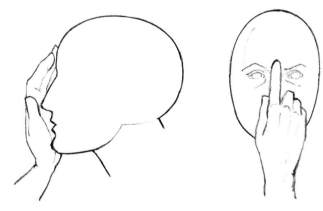

There are three different ways to sculpt hands. I suggest you try all of them.

Ball-built on a wire armature: Construct a wire armature as shown. Finger wires may be wrapped with a thin layer of florist's paper tape to provide a non-slip surface for clay. Roll ball shapes and put on finger wires in the same way as stringing beads. Add larger clay balls to rough in the palms and back of hand. Smooth and blend. This method is used for working with plasticine or wax sculpture and when the sculpture will be used to make a mold. Polymers and paperclays tend to slip on bare wire armatures. Incomplete blending of joints may also cause cracking or areas of weakness, leading to breakage. For these reasons, I recommend the other two methods instead.

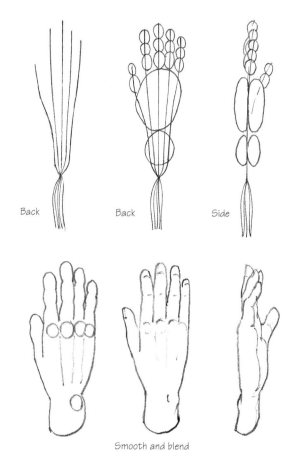

Sausage shaped: Roll long sausages of clay and press them together. Smooth and blend the hand back and the palm area. Bend the fingers into the desired position and sculpt the details. Add balls of clay for the knuckles and the pads of flesh on the palm. This method is quite simple to describe but requires sculpted detailing in order to be successful. A common failing among beginners is that they tend to stop at the sausage stage, so the resulting hand looks like an odd collection of boneless wieners.

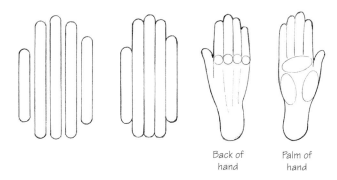

Back of hand   Palm of hand

Scissor-cut: I prefer the scissor-cut method, as it enables exact shaping without pressing. The principle of physics that for every action there is a reaction definitely applies to the polymer clays and, to a certain extent, to paperclay. Pressing on clays usually results in having to correct the other side.

Shape the clay into a paddle. With small fine-pointed scissors, make four cuts. If you use embroidery scissors, these cuts will usually arrange themselves into the arched finger shape of a real hand. Take the fattest outside slice and bend it over to the outside to make a thumb. Press the thumb into position forward of the palm. Remember, thumbs work in opposition to fingers when the hand is doing something. With your thumb and forefinger, pull and gently roll each of the fingers to smooth the scissor cuts and bring the fingers to the desired length. Now, with your knuckle, press into the palm.

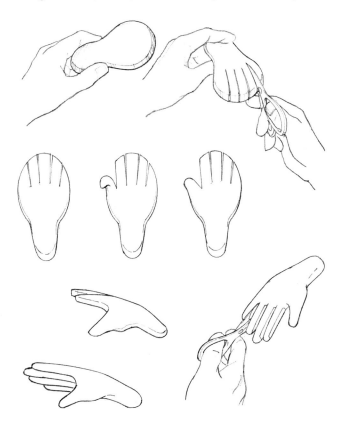

This will bend the back of the hand and give it the natural arch. Use scissors to trim fingers to uniform width, little finger a little thinner. Trim the ends of fingers so that the second finger is longer, index and third fingers are about equal in length, little finger reaches to second knuckle of third finger.

Observe the following features of your own hand in action. The fingers work in parallel and in tandem: when one moves, the others follow in a set pattern. When you grasp an object like a pen, the fingers not in direct use tend to curl under. When you grasp an object with thumb and fingers together, a depression is caused in the palm; the back of the hand narrows and arches more radically. Especially note that fingers are not particularly round in the adult hand. They are squarer, the result of the way the muscles and tendons fall along the sides of the finger. If you bend your finger fully, you will notice that two sharp angles are formed by the knuckles, like three sides of a square. Rounded parts of the fingers are on the inside tip pads and where the contraction of the finger creates puffs of skin between the knuckles. Remember, a human hand is never totally flat: the arm bones are nearly 2" thick at the wrist, but the base of the finger area is about 1" thick; the hand tapers from wrist to fingers. The tendons on the back of the hand cause the hand to slope downward to either side. The back of the palm area is a wedge, with the highest part at the wrist.

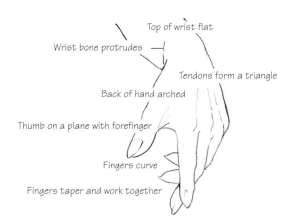

Top of wrist flat
Wrist bone protrudes
Tendons form a triangle
Back of hand arched
Thumb on a plane with forefinger
Fingers curve
Fingers taper and work together

Now, arrange the doll hand into the desired position. If you intend to have your doll hold an object, place that object in the hand at this point. Arrange the fingers to hold or use the object in a natural position. Hold the object in your own hand to check. Be prepared to check and re-check the position as you work.

When you bend the fingers into the desired position, the result is bent sausages. You need to create fingers with correctly positioned knuckles. To do this, you are going to snip off the fat on top of each finger. Each finger will be snipped three times lengthwise, knuckle to knuckle. Snip once on each finger to create the area between the base knuckle and the first knuckle, once to form the space between first and second knuckles, once more for the slightly tapered fingertip.

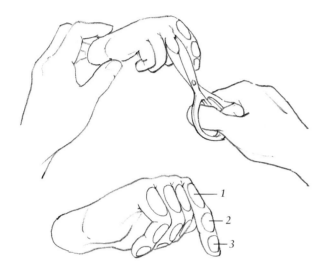

Check the position of the thumb, and snip along the top back to the base. Be sure the thumb and fingers you sculpt really can do the action you want.

Check the position of the hand with your own and, if tendons on the back of the hand are raised due to the position you want, add more clay to create that height.

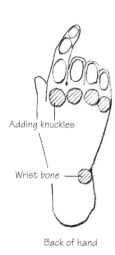

Adding knuckles

Wrist bone

Back of hand

On your own hand, check to see where rolls of flesh may be created by the desired position. If the hand is holding something, usually you will need to add one roll of clay to form a flesh roll at the base of the fingers. Add the flesh pad for the base of the thumb as needed. Add clay to square off the outside bottom of the palm. Now is the time to smooth the surfaces.

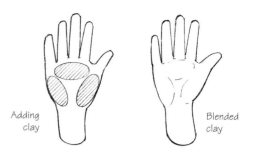

Adding clay

Blended clay

Palm of hand

Now to the other hand. Hands, of course, come in pairs. You will want to duplicate the size and the proportion of the first hand. Remember, however, that even though the hands will be the same size, if one is in an open finger position and the other is in a closed or holding position, the result is an illusion where the open one looks bigger.

As with all rules, there are exceptions! There are times when you can shape a hand to achieve artistic expression although it may not be in a natural position. An example of this is seen in the typical old-fashioned play doll hand where the two middle fingers are down and the forefinger and the little finger are turned up: a hand can do this, but not casually. The dramatic and expressive hand positions of dance make a figure more interesting *if* you have carefully combined them with the movement expressed in the figure as a whole.

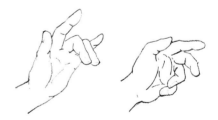

Further refinements to the hand, such as lines to show detail of the knuckles, fingernails, or added clay to define the veins below the flesh will depend on the maker's design decisions. As with faces, many artists become overly concerned with surface detail. Most hands, if in correct proportion and with the proper placement of bones and muscles, do not need additional detail unless the maker has decided to do an extremely realistic figure.

For either cloth-bodied dolls or wire-armatured figures, the hand should be extended above the wrist (or as much arm as will show outside the clothes), and a groove should be cut to hold the body fabric. Foil-covered wires can be inserted into polymer clays before final finishing of the hand. The wire can be cooked with no harm to the clay. If you want wires for paperclay hands, they should be aluminum or non-rusting. Alternatively, for paperclays, a hole can be made for wiring before drying.

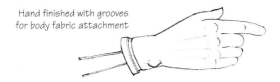

Hand finished with grooves for body fabric attachment

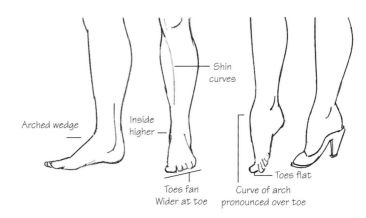

Arched wedge

Inside higher

Shin curves

Toes flat

Toes fan
Wider at toe

Curve of arch
pronounced over toe

FEET AND LEGS

When we get to the sculpture of the feet and legs, we come to a design decision. Will the doll have bare feet? Shoes made to fit? Sculpted shoes?

Bare feet: As with the faces and the hand sculpture, the foot has key points to remember. If the heel of the foot is placed against the chin, the tips of the toes will reach the hairline or top of the forehead. (Go on and try it: no one is looking. I can do it!) As with the hand, the bones and tendons are arranged so that the foot is higher or thicker at the ankle than at the toe. The foot is never flat on top. Think of it as a wedge where one side (the inside or arch) is higher. In a typical foot, the line is almost straight back-to-front on the arch. On the outside, the foot angles from the heel to the wider toe area. Ankle bones are important: when they can be located correctly, the rest of the foot follows. To locate the ankle bones, think baseball: the bone is "high inside" and "low on the outside." Big toes and little toes vary greatly in individuals, but usually the three middle toes are the same width. Also, don't forget that the toes fan, or form an arching pattern at the base, like the fingers. Toes do not come out in a straight-across manner. In most cases, you will want to sculpt the foot and the leg to the knee. Do notice that the shin bone curves from the inside, above the ankle bone, to the outside at the knee. Additionally, for the flesh of the calf, remember that "high outside, low inside" is true for the muscle structure.

High heels or tiptoe: When the foot is sculpted to wear or to show a high-heeled shoe, the shape of the foot changes radically. The toes stay flat, but the ankle comes forward so that it is nearly over the ball of the foot and the first knuckle joint of the big toe. This makes the arch assume a very pronounced curve. As the ankle comes forward, it pulls the leg along with it; this makes the leg almost a straight line from the knee to the toes, when you view it from the side.

Sculpting

For paperclay, it is recommended that you make a primary "bone" first. Bend and wrap non-rusting wire with foil and cover it with a layer of paperclay. On a figure of 18" and average proportions, the paperclay bone should not be thicker than ⅜". Let it dry thoroughly before you continue to sculpt. Or bend and wrap the wire as shown, adding paperclay a little at a time and allowing it to dry between layers.

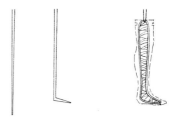

For polymer clays, wrap the wire with foil and bend it as shown. Build clay around the leg to form a big sausage.

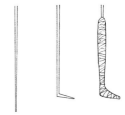

Then continue the sculpture, with either polymer or paperclay. Make a cut to form the instep. Make an angled cut to form the arch (A). Make cuts at either side of the back of the foot to form the heel (B). Make a cut to form the front of the foot wedge (C). Place the ankle bones by cutting away the area above on each side of the ankle (D, E) and trimming to narrow the ankle above the ankle bones and below the calf (F, G). Model the calf so that the flesh is correctly placed (H–J). With your fingers or a tool, pull a curved line to suggest the shin curve (K). Smooth and blend cut areas to shape the legs.

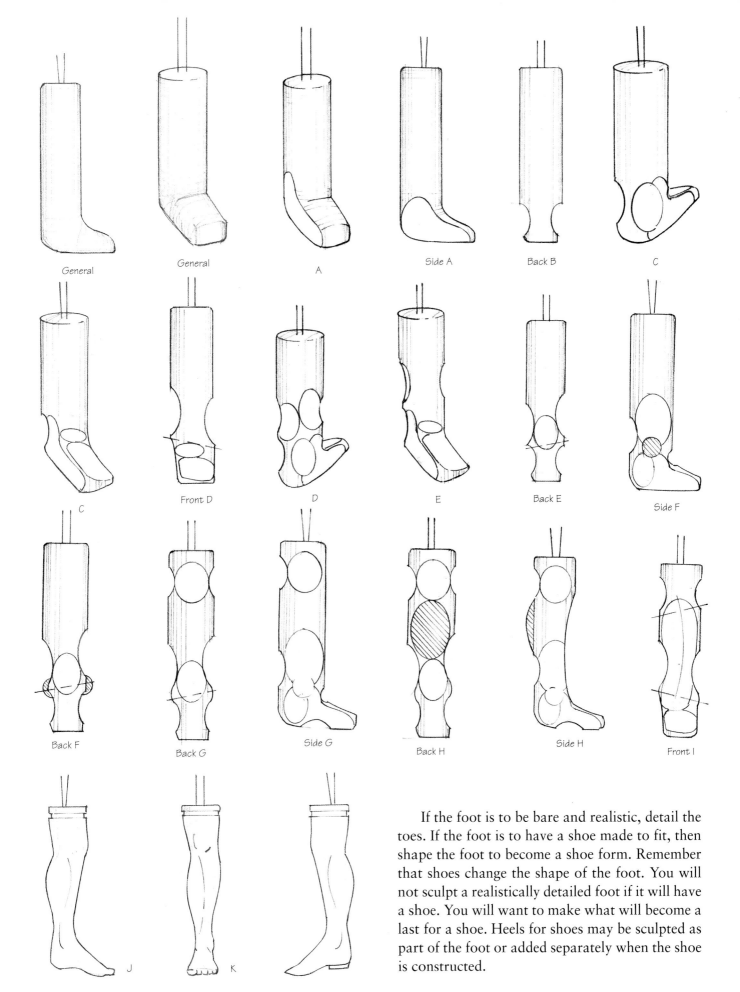

General

General

A

Side A

Back B

C

C

Front D

D

E

Back E

Side F

Back F

Back G

Side G

Back H

Side H

Front I

J

K

If the foot is to be bare and realistic, detail the toes. If the foot is to have a shoe made to fit, then shape the foot to become a shoe form. Remember that shoes change the shape of the foot. You will not sculpt a realistically detailed foot if it will have a shoe. You will want to make what will become a last for a shoe. Heels for shoes may be sculpted as part of the foot or added separately when the shoe is constructed.

If you want to sculpt shoes rather than feet, continue to finish in the design of your choice. It helps if you can check your work against a real foot in a similar shoe. Be sure not to forget to give height and shape to the arch of the foot so it looks like there are real bones inside the shoe. Shoe buttons or beads may be imbedded in the clay and dried or cured with it.

PREPARATION FOR CURING

All good dollmaking includes a large portion of "thinking ahead" and anticipating potential problems. In the case of materials which will cure or dry hard, there are several areas where you might want to add specialized treatment before the material hardens.

1. Be sure to consider how your figure will be assembled on the body. For bodies with wire armatures or stuffed cloth, parts will need to be grooved so that body-covering fabric can be gathered and attached to the sculpted parts. The only exception would be a figure with a breastplate. A breastplate can be attached either by gluing it to the stuffed body or by making holes and sewing or using tape ties. Before curing, read the chapter on curing (page 41) and prepare your sculpted pieces according to your choice of body type. Also, refer back to the illustrations on pages 16–17.

2. Wigging: In most cases, simple dolls are wigged by gluing on a purchased doll wig. As you become more specialized in your doll characters, you might wish to try rooting hair into the clay. Depending on the material, this can usually be done before curing. Experiment. You might also want to consider making the holes for rooting after curing. Another way to attach wigging material is to use tanned animal hides with hair still attached, or pile fabrics. In such cases, you will get a better fit if the skull is carved away $1/16$" or less (as if the scalp were removed) in the area where material will be glued on. In this way, the fabric or the skin will be level with the head, and the hair will appear to grow out of it naturally. Heads may also be grooved along the part in the hair style. This allows the hair to be glued into the groove so that it will appear to rise naturally on either side of the part.

3. For solid jointed dolls made of polymer clays, the joint holes or attachment areas should be sculpted before curing. Although these clays can be drilled when cured, there is some risk that a drill bit could slip or the material be too thin to take the stress of a hole. Paperclay, on the other hand, should be drilled *after* it has thoroughly dried.

4. In most cases, for wire-armatured figures, you have already set wires in the hands and feet as you sculpted. You will need to provide a hole through the neck, up into the head. Usually, the hole made by your working armature or holding stick will do. Be sure the hole is big enough and deep enough into the head to take four widths of 16-gauge wire. Again, this can be drilled out after curing, but it is more efficient to do it before. Doing so also reduces the risk of cracking the cured material with the drill or cutting tool.

One last word about sculpture! Do not rush to cure your material. Oh, it looks wonderful! Golly, you feel great! However, it is surprising how many "boo-boos" you will notice if you let it sit for a while. I keep my finished work on a shelf above my desk; it stays there at least a week before I decide that I have found everything that needs correction. Keep your work in a safe place where you can see it in the course of your daily activities. Move it two or three times to other locations, so you can see it from different angles.

Sign and copyright your sculpture before cooking by incising the copyright mark, your name, and the year. Traditionally, this is done on the back of the head or on the neck: © Mary Jane Dollmaker, 1994.

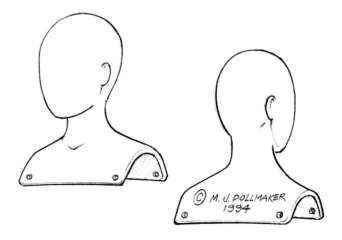

# CURING

When I began this book, I suspected that my approaches to "engineering" the clays were fairly conservative, compared with my colleagues. Sticking fairly close to the manufacturers' directions, I have few problems in curing the clays. But, my creations are sculpture and character delineation, in costume and pose. I paint my clay surfaces fully, so I have never needed to do much experimentation with mixing products, colors, or curing techniques to achieve specific flesh tones. When I asked other artists how they proceed, I found about half work pretty much as I do. The rest do all kinds of interesting things, and they were very willing to share a few tips and tricks which appear in this section and the next.

PAPERCLAYS

Paperclays (Creative Paperclay, La Doll, Celluclay) start the curing process the minute the package is opened, when the moist product is exposed to air. There is no great mystery of technique involved in curing paperclay. Your job in working with the paperclays is to stop the natural curing process until you have completed the sculpture and you are ready to let it dry. It will pay to understand how the product reacts to air over the period of drying, as this can affect how you work. The following descriptions apply most specifically to Creative Paperclay, but the basic techniques and effects are approximately the same for all these products.

Suppose you have modeled your sculpture over a foil or Styrofoam® ball, and the paperclay is about ¼" thick. If you leave that, it might appear dry in 8 to 12 hours. However, even when the exterior of a piece looks and feels dry, the interior may be quite wet. Three or four days later, you could cut into the piece or remove the core and find the interior still quite damp. This is, in part, because the dry exterior surface serves to seal in moisture. I have talked to artists who modeled over foil or foam, dried overnight, painted and finished the surface in the following 48 hours. This worries me, as I have found that even a hollowed-out piece, where air can freely circulate to the interior, can take up to three days

to dry completely. Therefore, be very aware of how long it might take to dry the interior of your pieces, and do not go on to finish and seal the work until you are positive it is *thoroughly* dry.

Since the paperclay is drying from the outside to the inside, it forms a slow crust. If you work on the dry surface, you will find that this crust can peel off. You will also find that the crust is rubbery. It is not unusual during this period to have the surface crack and the whole piece bend at the same time. To avoid problems like this, do not attempt to re-work sculpture until you are sure that it has thoroughly dried.

One positive aspect of paperclay is that it can be moistened and re-sculpted after being dried. Just take your time. I prefer to keep my work very wet until I am totally satisfied with the sculpture. Then I let it dry thoroughly. When it is thoroughly dried, I re-work, clean, patch, or repair as needed.

An alternative approach is to build the paperclay sculpture over the armature very slowly, letting each layer dry before you add the next. If you apply multiple thin layers, when you are ready to let the piece finally dry, only the top layer will need drying. This method requires infinite patience and a very fine knowledge of anatomy. The time involved will be about the same with either approach. I generally use this method for sculpting arms and legs, since it allows me to create a hard bone of paperclay to build on.

In either the wet or dry approaches with paperclay, no matter how careful you are, the material is exposed to air as you work. The exposed surface will always be drying. The material will even be drawn dry by your hands as you work it. This is why you keep a spray bottle of water handy. Just a quick squirt from time to time—not a soaking—will keep material workable.

Just because paperclay tends to dry once it is out of the package does not mean you have to work fast. You can keep work in process for days and weeks if you keep it damp while you are working and cover it well when you are not. Usually, a tight cover of plastic wrap or a thin plastic bag will keep a piece moist for a day or two. Check and spray with water if necessary after no more than two days.

When your piece is ready for final drying, remember that paperclay pieces can warp while drying. This is not necessarily due to the material itself; often it is the result of span, gravity, and uneven downward pressure or weight that the piece exerts on itself. If a leg is laid on its side with no support, an ankle could bend out of the sculpted line. The same is possible with parts like arms, wrists, and breastplates. You will need to consider this and prop pieces wherever they could sag.

Paperclay can be dried in open air on a wire rack. The process can be speeded up by using a fan, drying outside when temperatures are above 70° F with low humidity, or drying in a warm oven. When oven-drying, leave the door open so that moisture can escape. I often dry my paperclay pieces on top of my air-cleaner fan box; other artists use furnaces, light bulbs, and hair dryers. Whichever method you choose, the piece is dry when it feels dry, not cold, almost as light as Styrofoam, and is white. Remember: *warm, light,* and *white.*

Sagging or cracking that might occur during drying can be easily corrected. If a large area needs to be fixed, rough up the surface with sandpaper or a file, moisten, and add wet paperclay. If a crack occurs, mix paperclay with water to a paste and fill in. Breakage is rare: dry paperclay is extremely strong, even in thin areas. Small finger tips can break off, but only under considerable force. A clean break can usually be repaired more efficiently with craft or wood glue than by trying to re-build the area with paperclay.

I have not used Celluclay much myself, except for interior structures and accessories. Dollmakers who regularly use it warn about shrinkage and suggest that it is a good idea to sculpt both arms or legs at the same time, so that if any shrinkage occurs, it will be fairly uniform in both pieces.

POLYMER CLAYS

All of the polymer clays—Sculpey, Super Sculpey, Fimo, and Cernit—are cured by heating them to 275° F for not less than 10 minutes in a home oven. Personal preferences for times and temperatures vary according to the size of the piece and the artist's experiences. It seems to be a general rule that most dollmakers prefer to cure their pieces longer: up to an hour in some cases. I find that most of my pieces are sufficiently cured between 15 and 20 minutes at 275°.

What can cook? You would be surprised what objects doll artists have cooked in their polymer pieces. Some cook the material used for hair and fabric body coverings. Some cure bare legs, cover them with stockings and sculpted shoes, then cook again to cure the shoes. A few routinely cure their clays with glass, plastic, or pre-cooked clay eyes. Some have had success with this, while others have had set-in eyes pop right out of the head. It seems that the only limit is the melting or flash point of the material.

Because of fumes, curing Styrofoam inside clay is *definitely not recommended.* Plastic, vinyl, or resin-based materials contain chemicals that may give off fumes when they are heated to a certain temperature. These fumes can be toxic! They won't just smell bad; they will knock you out—or worse—before you have time to think about it! Don't put anything in the oven that could cause a fire or create poisonous fumes. If you are in any doubt about the material you intend to cook, ask your local fire marshal.

By the way, don't think you can end-run the Styrofoam danger by totally surrounding Styrofoam with the clay. Good try, but fumes are fumes. If you cannot be made to fear fumes, be afraid of losing your hard-earned sculpture. Styrofoam expands when heated and will often cause the surrounding clay to crack and blister. *Just forget Styrofoam.*

OVENS

I prefer and recommend a regular home oven. Gas or electric, it makes no difference as long as you can control the temperature. Toaster ovens will work, but most dollmakers report that heating is uneven and unreliable with them. Steamers, crock pots, counter-top ovens and the like can work <u>in theory</u>, but in actual practice you will find that you will not have the needed steady temperature control.

The Microwave

Sooner or later, some creative doll artist had to try it. If you think a minute, you can save yourself the effort and the waste. A microwave oven works on the principle of exciting the molecules until they get hot enough to cook. Most microwave ovens do not create what we could call "even excitement." Some parts of an item will cook, and others will not: consider the microwaved baked potato. Polymer clays cooked in the microwave have been known to cook unevenly, creating a melt-down on certain portions of a piece; some artists report that pieces have blown up. Use a regular oven; don't waste your time and your work.

Oven Temperatures

We all know (if we can remember the lost art of cooking) that ovens can "cook hot" or "cook low" relative to the thermostat setting. That is, an oven set at 350° F might actually heat to 365°. Get a separate oven thermometer and check your oven. Many have a setting screw for adjusting temperatures and thermostats. See your manufacturer's instructions or call a dealer, if necessary. Depending on the amount of material in the oven and the size of the cooking surface, heat flow can be restricted. For instance, if you have put in a whole cookie sheet of parts, the sheet is taking up the majority of the rack space, and heat from the element below flows around the sheet unevenly or is stopped, making it hotter than you want it to be.

Polymer Curing

Let's take a minute to consider what is actually going to happen with this polymer clay when it goes in the oven. It is not at all like kiln firing of water-based ceramic clays, where the process is similar to fusing sand to make glass. In her book *The New Clay*, Nan Roche includes a very elegant chapter on the chemical components and heat reactions of the polymer clays. Everyone using the materials will benefit by reading her description. For us, here, it will suffice to know that the clays are made up of polymer resins and plasticizing agents in a suspension which will stay unstable or soft unless it is heated to a degree where molecular fusion will take place. When that temperature is reached and maintained long enough to make the whole piece (and all its molecules) fuse, then we have a hard, cured piece of polymer clay sculpture. It is also important to know that, if the piece does not reach a uniform heat, some parts will not fuse thoroughly. Think pork: polymer clays need to reach a specific temperature in order to be considered cooked and usable.

COOKING UTENSILS

Any ovenproof glass dish will do; I have even used wooden boards. I prefer a glass baking dish; metal tends to get hotter and to concentrate the heat on the parts of the pieces lying against it, and the manufacturer doesn't recommend it. The smooth surface of the glass also makes it just that much less likely for the pieces to be marred or marked. The pan or dish should be no larger than half the size of the oven baking rack. You do not want a wall-to-wall cookie sheet that would restrict air flow in the oven. The utensils should also be used *only* for cooking your sculpture: do *not* use the same pans and dishes for family food. This is a good way to use chipped dishes that you might have had to throw out anyhow.

For the record, suspending pieces by their wires from the oven racks did not work for me: when pieces reach high heat, they tend to sag. For the same reason, just laying pieces on wire baking racks does not work either.

LOADING THE OVEN

I have a tendency to save cooking until I have two or three sets of parts ready to go into the oven. It takes a little thought to lay them out for best effect. Heads with flange necks can sit upright. Heads with breastplates can lie face up. Depending on the configuration of the head and neck, I sometimes support the back of the neck with a small scrap of dowel. You can also use a lump of clay; if it sticks, remove with a gentle twist. I have also left the head on the working armature for cooking; however, you must be sure to give the head a good twist to make sure it is loosened from the nail or dowel support. As a general rule, anything cooked inside the clay will tend to be stuck fast.

When the pieces are cooked, you will notice that the side that touches the baking sheet will be slightly glazed and, in some cases, flattened slightly. You will want to make sure that arms and legs are laid so that there is minimal contact, and that contact is in places easy to clean up. I have tried laying pieces on soft Polyfil® stuffing: some doll artists do this routinely. However, I have found that I do not like the little bits of lint that get stuck in the clay. It seems better to avoid oven glazing by covering the baking surface with parchment paper. Underlining with foil can cause browning from the additional reflected heat.

Generally, lay hands so that the little finger side is touching the sheet. Lay legs so that the instep touches the sheet. Some ankles may need extra support with dowel blocking. Ordinarily, hands that lie on their outside edges will not need any extra support for fingers. When you place the sheet in the oven, make sure that nothing has rolled or shifted and that no pieces are on top of wires. Double check the oven temperature dial. Close the door *gently!*

COOKING POLYMER CLAYS

Your pieces and your oven will make every case an experiment. Every type of polymer clay, and even different packages of the same type, can cure differently. You will need to observe your own results and adjust accordingly. I can only tell you what works in general.

Package instructions indicate that the clay can be cooked up to 20 minutes at 275° F. I have found that a head that has been built over foil, no larger than 2½" tall, will cook in 15 minutes. I pre-heat the oven to 275° and put the pieces in as quickly as possible, so that heat does not escape. I set my oven timer for 15 minutes. When the 15 minutes are up, I turn the oven off but leave the door closed. Pieces cool in the oven until they are entirely cool to the touch. If I have any doubt that the pieces are thoroughly cured, I will repeat the whole process again.

There are reasons for allowing pieces to cool entirely before checking that they are done. One of the big problems of first-time users is, "My pieces are soft," or "How come I can't get my stuff to cook hard?" Polymer clays do not set until they are cool. If you touch them right out of the hot oven, they will be soft. Poke them with a fingernail and you will leave a good mark. Most damage to your pieces and to your hands happens when you try to move, touch, or test pieces while they are still hot. Just-cooked pieces *will* be extremely hot: they can burn your fingers. If you must touch, use a pot holder or oven mitt. Allowing pieces to cool in the oven as the heat is slowly dissipated also prevents the cracking that could happen in going from hot oven to cooler outside air.

If the pieces are still soft and crumbly (test on the inside of head or neck) when they are totally cooled, you can re-cook them. Follow the same procedure: 15 minutes with the oven on, then cooling in the oven. Larger pieces, heads 3" in diameter and more, can be cooked for an initially longer period. If a large piece does not have small protrusions, it can stay in an oven set at 275° for up to 30 minutes with no damage. Always go slowly and check temperatures. My old oven did not have a good door seal, so the oven would cycle on and get hotter more frequently. This caused some scorching on small protrusions like noses and ears. My current oven is very tight. Once the set temperature is reached, it will not cycle on more than once in 10 minutes. Learn your oven's idiosyncrasies.

ADDING ON

I suppose I should say a word about adding raw material to cured material. It can be done. I have done it. It has worked. Somehow, I have never been very happy with the results in my own work, so it is not something I do regularly. Many artists, however, routinely sculpt and cure several times before they have completed a piece. I notice that many of these artists also complain about cracks, browning, and crumbling. Is there a connection? Very possibly. I recommend that you complete your sculpture as much as you can before curing. Use the add-on and re-cook process only to repair or make necessary changes.

CURING RECIPES

Dollmakers are fairly cautious souls. They generally vary from the box instructions only on the side of less risk: lower temperatures and longer times. Most indicate that this makes them feel their cured pieces will reach a maximum cure strength with less cracking and the least likelihood of browning.

Manufacturers' instructions give you *average safe* parameters of time and precisely verified oven temperatures. They cannot foresee what an experimental artist might do as far as mixing products, concocting specific interior armature structures, or what each one's desired finished look might be. Neither can I. If you decide to mix products or colors, proceed with caution and be prepared to learn from mistakes!

Here are suggestions from some artists:

Carol Nordell:
Super Sculpey mixed with Sculpey III Translucent, 40 minutes for a 15" figure at 250°, cool in oven.

Kathy Gunson:
Super Sculpey, 1 hour at 225°, cure small touch-up additions 8-10 minutes with a hair dryer.

Jane Covington:
Combined brands of polymer clays, cushioned on Polyfil stuffing, 1 hour at 250°. This can be repeated several times.

Marilyn Radzat:
Super Sculpey, or mixture of Fimo and Super Sculpey, 20 minutes at 300°.

Maureen Carlson:
Fimo, 30 minutes at 250° and then 265° for 45 minutes for strength.

Jodi and Richard Creager:
Super Sculpey, 17 minutes at 250°, check and bake exactly 3 more minutes, cool out of oven covered with cloth.

Kathryn Walmsley:
Cernit over Super Sculpey, bake at 250°, cool in oven. Add-ons, bake 10 minutes, cool, bake another 10 minutes and cool.

Randi Taylor:
3 parts Fimo Flesh, 1 part Cernit Flesh: 25 to 30 minutes at 275°-300°.

Candy Hund:
Mix 1 part Fimo Flesh with 1 part Fimo Transparent, bake slightly lower than package directions, cool in oven.

Linda Kertzman:
3 parts Cernit, 1 part Sculpey, convection oven 250°-300°. Adding Sculpey seems to eliminate flecks in Cernit.

Bob and Ann Ross Anderson:
Super Sculpey, pre-heat oven to 275°, cook 20-30 minutes on tissue paper in glass dish, cool in oven.

Pat Kolesar:
Fimo, 10-15 minutes at 225°, cool completely and cook again for the same amount of time.

Bill Nelson:
Super Sculpey or Cernit, 250° for 20 minutes.

Pat Brooks:
Solved cracking problems by cooling in refrigerator.

Painting your doll is a matter of personal choice and desired effect. No two artists will follow exactly the same processes in painting or finishing a doll. There are few specific how-to methods. There are, however, some basics to consider when choosing a finish. Generally, if you are in a mood to experiment, do it on scraps or on the back of the head, where a wig will cover it.

PAPERCLAYS

Paperclay is a wonderful material for the artist who likes to paint, because it can take just about any surface treatment. You can create a very soft watercolor effect or a highly rendered effect, a very smooth polished or lacquered look, or a waxed finish: anything goes.

Paperclay is *paper* and is subject to damp conditions. Almost any painting technique can be used to finish a paperclay surface as long as it is well sealed. Paperclay can revert to a soggy mass if it becomes too wet. While a doll will probably not become thoroughly soaked, it may pick up moisture in very humid conditions if it is not well sealed.

Cleaning: Do not attempt to sand paperclay until it is thoroughly dry. The material will then smooth nicely with very fine sandpaper. Take care to move the sandpaper in different directions to get even wear. Sand very lightly, as pressure can remove the surface. If you want a very smooth surface, after sanding you can go over the whole piece with a wet paint brush. This will usually make a very satisfactory, finely toothed paint-ready finish when dry. One merit of this product is that you can go back and work on it again and again. Wet material can be added at any point and re-sanded, if needed.

Watercolor: Being paper, it takes very well to a watercolor effect. If paints are applied directly to the raw surface, it will react like watercolor paper, absorbing the paint. The surface will swell slightly. Care must be taken to avoid puddling or blotting of color washes over the surface when you paint flesh tones or cheek color. The

paperclay surface can be prepared with an undercoat of gesso to prevent puddling but, if so, the final effect will be somewhat opaque.

Acrylics or oils: The surface can be painted to achieve the effect of a highly rendered oil painting. First apply two or three coats of gesso under acrylic paints, or up to six well-sanded coats of gesso under oil paints.

Lacquer and spray paints: Paperclay can achieve the look of older composition dolls. In fact, it has been used successfully for repair. If this effect is desired, be sure parts are sanded as smooth as possible. Any surface irregularity will show or will take many coats to cover. Apply three to six coats of gesso, sanding and smoothing after each coat. Apply lacquer or spray paints in thin coats until the surface is uniform and smooth. Be sure the surface is completely dry before painting features.

Sealing: All paperclay pieces should be well sealed inside and out with a clear sealer or clear matte spray. Some artists prefer to seal the cleaned surface and then paint; some prefer to do all painting and then seal. If you have used pastels, chalks, or powdered make-up in your coloring, *test* before using a sealer. Sometimes, these dry, powdery materials will run when sprayed with a sealer. If you have used a gesso undercoating and acrylic paints, or a wax or glaze, it is unlikely that more sealer will be necessary on the surface. However, if any parts have been hollowed, those interior surfaces should be sealed. Basically, you want to make sure all surfaces, interior and exterior, are covered.

POLYMER CLAYS

In finishing polymer clays, almost anything goes *except* oils or lacquer-based paints applied directly to the surface. Directly applied lacquer-based paints will not dry. Some sealers will not dry when directly applied to the surface: the lacquers interact with the polymer resins and soften them. Sealers on polymer pieces are used only to keep paint from being chipped or disturbed by water. If you are thinking of using a sealer, be sure to test it on cured scrap material. Sculpey, Cernit, and Fimo product lines do include glazes and matte sealers created especially for use on their products. Experiment to see if you like the effect before applying it to your finished piece.

Most artists' oil paints require an absorbent ground in order to dry. I have, on one or two occasions, successfully used oil and lacquer-based paints on polymer clays, but only on surfaces prepared with several coats of gesso. If you like to paint with oils, I recommend that you consider using paperclay as your sculpting medium.

Preparation: I cannot overstress the need for making the sculpture as clean and smooth as possible before curing. If you have done this and repaired any oven problems, your pieces are essentially ready to paint. Some artists do sand polymer clay pieces, but I have found that sanding roughs and dulls the surface unnecessarily. If surface problems remain after curing, you can try rubbing with a piece of lint-free cotton soaked in a bit of acetone or fingernail polish remover. This will re-melt the surface slightly and allow small blemishes to be smoothed out. Do beware of using linty materials when rubbing with solvents. Little fibers will be fused into the softened clay when it re-hardens—most frustrating if you are painting the surface or if you want a clean clay surface. On Sculpey figures, for minor cleaning in tiny areas, such as between fingers, a scrub with powdered kitchen cleanser and an old toothbrush will take care of small irregularities. When I sand, carve, or use a softening material to prepare Sculpey surfaces for full painting, I always wash and dry the pieces before going on. This helps provide a dust-free surface.

There are two preferences for finishing polymer clays. Some artists paint only the features and highlight colors on the cured medium, without any flesh-tone painting. This is usually the standard approach for Fimo and Cernit, as those clays are packaged pre-colored or can be mixed to get nice cured flesh tones. White Sculpey is commonly given a full surface painting. Flesh-tone painting on Super Sculpey varies, depending on the color as packaged. Super Sculpey can range from almost cream-colored to tan to pink-ish-gray as it comes from the box.

Highlight and feature painting: Companies recommend their own paints, or you can apply acrylic paints with a fine brush. Some artists prefer to sculpt the white of the eye in white clay material. Some use pastels and powder-based cosmetics for detailing shadows and cheek colors.

Full surface painting: Acrylic paints are by nature thick. Applied directly from the tube or bottle, they essentially create a layer of plastic on top of your doll. This layer can be peeled off. To prevent thickness and potential peel, I prepare the surface with several coats of gesso thinned to the consistency of milk. The first few coats will be uneven; it takes at least four coats to achieve a smooth undercoat. This undercoat, if applied in multiple thin layers, will not be as likely to peel, nor will it appear thick. Even when painting with acrylics, I prefer a lighter, almost opaque watercolor effect. For this, I paint six to eight very thin coats of diluted gesso. When the gesso covers satisfactorily, I apply two or three very light coats of flesh-colored acrylic thinned with water. This produces a chalky, matte look. If you prefer a solid, opaque, almost shiny look, flesh-colored acrylic paints may be applied after the gesso undercoat has made a smooth cover. The artist who uses this method will usually begin to mix in colors and render the flesh tones after first applying a solid base flesh color.

WAX-OVER

For over a hundred years, there has been "something about the look of wax." It does tend to soften and give a glow to any doll face—that added human feel. Paperclays and polymer clays can all be wax-coated. You will need a container big enough to submerge the parts completely. Best is a three-pound coffee can. You will also need paraffin, from the canning section of your grocery. Candle-making wax from a craft supplier will also work. It requires a double boiler in order to protect you from a flash fire: you want water between the hot wax and flame or electric element. For larger pieces, over very slow heat, place a frying pan filled with water. Place a coffee can in the water and melt paraffin slowly. You will need to fill the can with wax to the height of the doll part: if the head is 3", you will need 3" of wax. You will need at least 2" of additional container height to allow for displacement. (Check first with *water* in the container.) In this example, you need a container 5" deep. While the wax is melting, place the parts to be dipped in a warm oven. Wax will make a lighter coating on warm parts and is less likely to build up in tiny areas such as eye, nose, and mouth corners. When the wax is melted, use tongs or armature wires extending from the piece to hold it during dipping. Dip heads quickly and turn them face up quickly, so that wax runs off to the back of the head. Hold the part in the air for a minute to allow the wax to set. Lay the piece down gently on a glass sheet to complete cooling. When the wax has cooled, use a pin or needle to clean excess wax from sculpted corners and over the eyes.

BASICS FOR FINISHING ALL MEDIUMS

- Make sure the sculpture is as smooth as possible before painting.
- Clean up any dings and repair them before painting.
- Prepare surfaces to receive full flesh-tone paint with gesso.
- Be sure to seal paperclay.
- Always test any paint or sealer on scrap clay before applying it to a doll.

RECIPES

The following will give you an idea of the many ways artists go about creating, painting, and highlighting the features of their dolls.

Patricia Dugré Bibb: Paperclay can be sculpted over a stuffed cotton body, covered with three coats of gesso. Paperclay is applied to a slightly damped gesso surface.

Toni Carroll: Cernit Flesh and Fimo #71 Bronze make a nice ethnic skin tone.

Jane Covington: Very nice black flesh can be obtained by adding 3-4 packages of terra cotta and ¼–½ package of black Fimo to one pound of flesh-colored clay.

Maureen Carlson: For a nice flesh, mix a marble-sized piece of terra cotta Fimo with a 12 oz. package of flesh pink Fimo.

Betts Vidal: Detail unpainted Fimo with Pigma® pens.

Pat Kolesar: No-fire china paints for wash, blush with red china paint. Detail with acrylics.

Linda Wingerd-Graham: Color with cosmetics—eyeshadows, highlighters, and blushers are wonderful colorants for dolls. They are already in a useful variety of skin tones and much finer grained than pastels. Easier to blend colors, don't look plastic like heavy acrylic, and you can get more variety of shadings.

Scott Gray: Liquid acrylics blended with gesso, with a final glaze of very diluted Jewelry Glaze™.

Gisele Hanson: Prime with gesso, paint surface with acrylics, highlight cheeks with artists' oils (blend well with fingers), and use a high-gloss sealant over eyes.

Betsey Baker: For Celluclay or Paperclay, prime with two coats of gesso, followed by two coats of Liquitex Artist Color sandalwood thinned with water. Before the second coat is dry, work in burnt sienna, naphthol crimson medium, cobalt blue, cadmium yellow light, and blend for flesh tones. All colors mixed with base coat of sandalwood. All coats applied thinly. Works well on Sculpey, too. Gesso base is important, as Celluclay unsealed will swell if acrylic paints are used.

Toni Carroll: Use a stylus to burnish the surface of paperclay to get it as smooth as possible before painting.

Paul Robbins: Burnish Paperclay with a bit of dampened suede.

Carol Nordell: Use rubbing alcohol to smooth unbaked clay. Use a mixture of rubbing alcohol and baby oil after sanding the baked doll.

Barbara Lady: Prior to painting, wash sculpted pieces with dish detergent and water, and rinse well.

George Stuart: The skin, where exposed, is done with an airbrush and is composed of ground pigments, talc, matting agent, binder, bottled water, a wetting agent, and perhaps a few drops of alcohol.

Marjory by E. J. Taylor
28", Sculpey with Celluclay body
Photo by Sloane Bosniak

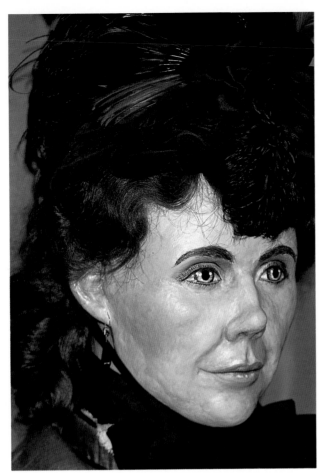

Prudence by Betsey Baker
60", Celluclay and cloth over wire armature
Photo by Betsey Baker

Amy by Ellen Poitras
16", Super Sculpey, jointed body of Super Sculpey and wood
Photo by Nancy Walters

The Innkeeper's Wife (from *Les Misérables*) by Robert McKinley
17", Paperclay and cloth over wire armature
Photo by Robert McKinley

Heron Woman—A Story Keeper
by Maureen Carlson
14", Fimo and cloth
Photo by Maureen Carlson

Maya Prince by George Stuart
18", Sculpey and Paperclay over armature
Photo by Peter D'Aprix

Sarah—Feed the Birds by Judith Klawitter
20", Super Sculpey, cloth over wire armature
Photo by Mark Bryant

Hagglinda by Jodi and Richard Creager
15", Super Sculpey
Photo by Richard Creager

Grandfather Earth by Dee Shaughnessy
15", Sculpey
Photo by Dee Shaughnessy

Shalani by Susan Dunham
6", Paperclay
Photo by Susan Dunham

Mother Earth by Kathryn Walmsley
19", Cernit and cloth over wire armature
Photo by Kathryn Walmsley

Thomas Trickster by Susanna Oroyan
27", Paperclay
Photo by W. Donald Smith

Manon by Lilian Tolido-Elzer
19", Paperclay
Photo by Gerard Tolido

Angel by Marilyn Radzat
34", Fimo and cloth over wire armature
Photo by R. Sondgrath

Young Musician by Linda Kertzman
12", Cernit
Photo by Jack Cole

Cinderella's Stepmother by Transcendence
(Margaret Finch and Marta Finch-Kozlosky)
16", Super Sculpey on wire armature
Photo by Lynton Gardiner

Detail of *Cinderella's Stepmother*
Photo by Marta Finch-Kozlosky

Zachariah Cullen—Mountain Man by Linda Wingerd-Graham
19", Fimo, Cernit, and cloth over wire armature
Photo by W. Donald Smith

African Woman—Going to Market by Linda Lunsford Elder
20", Super Sculpey and cloth over wire armature
Photo by W. Donald Smith

Sioux Dancer by Annie Wahl
12", cloth over wire armature
Photo by W. Donald Smith

Queen of Miami Beach by Nancy Walters
14", Paperclay
Photo by Nancy Walters

Cousin Millie by Susanna Oroyan
18", Sculpey
Photo by W. Donald Smith

Gertrude by Holly Conrad
17", Super Sculpey
Photo by Joe Parker

Birthday Girl by Hedy Katin
40", DAS® face sculpture covered with
polyester knit fabric, stuffed cloth body
Photo by Hedy Katin

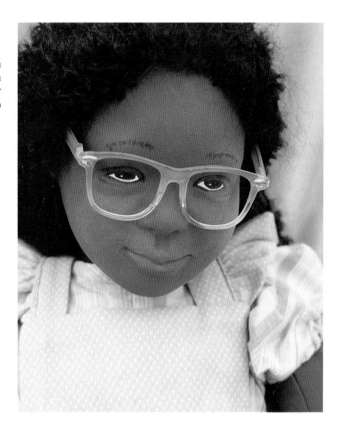

The 18th Empress by Susanna Oroyan
18", Sculpey
Photo by W. Donald Smith

Rodney Safemedows—Ventriloquist Figure by Ray Munger
60", composition
Photo by Sears, Roebuck & Company

Clown—Red Shoes by Barbara Lady
14", Fimo
Photo by W. Donald Smith

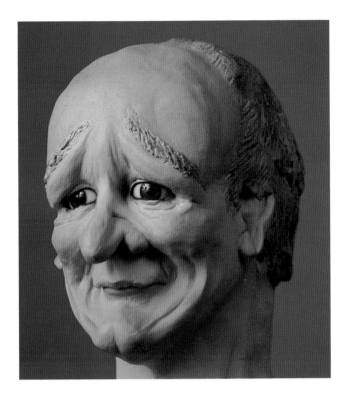

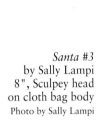

Male Head
by Nancy Cronin
6", Claystone®
Photo by Al Pererio

Santa #3
by Sally Lampi
8", Sculpey head
on cloth bag body
Photo by Sally Lampi

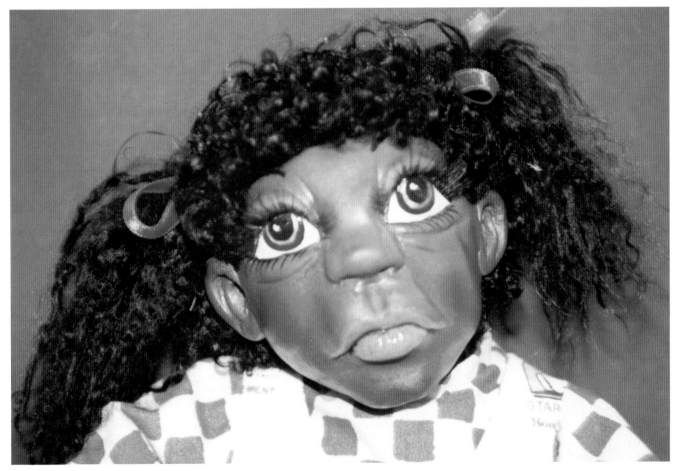

Proud Lucy by Pat Kolesar
18", hand-poured vinyl
Photo by Donald Kolesar

Father Christmas by Rosemary Volpi
24", Super Sculpey, cloth over wire armature
Photo by Sam Schumacher

Annemieke and *Hilda* by Marleen Engeler
30" and 33", Cernit
Photo by Meindert L. Wentzel

CONSTRUCTING BODIES

GENERAL

If there is a part of dollmaking I dislike, it is making the body. With most of my dolls, which begin as a set of sculpted parts, I have to do *something* to hook all the parts together. However, the structure while in progress just doesn't thrill me, but the process must be done, and done well, because I know that the body and the movement of the piece can make or ruin the doll as a completed and successful piece. The greatest sculpture and the most fantastic costuming will not amount to anything if they are hung on a poorly thought-out body. Notice that I did not say "poorly constructed": in this area, as with all of dollmaking, if you think it out well, it will construct well.

While you are sculpting, you will have already made a decision about the body. Some of us are inclined to like sculpture and the beauty of the human form, so we will create our dolls to show as much of that as possible. This type of doll is usually sculpted as a solid piece and then cut apart to make joints for movement. Artists who prefer body work could be easily content to do a figurine (fixed, unmovable figure), but they do jointing as a token recognition of the doll idea.

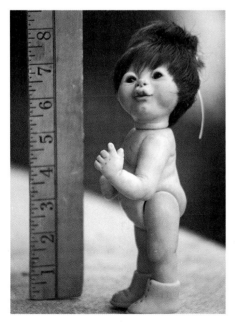

Bitsy sculpted in Fimo by Pat Kolesar, 8" fully jointed figure with sculpted shoes
Photo by Donald Kolesar

Some artists are enamored of the idea of human motion. They love the idea of the play of the muscles and tendons, and the action of the joints. These artists tend to become immersed in the problems of engineering joints close to the nature of the real human. Some of their results are, indeed, feats of engineering very close to divine.

Most dollmakers who choose to work in polymer or paperclay do so because they like the idea of expressing character. They are more interested in creating a costumed miniature human replica than a dressable play doll. Therefore, they do not have a great need to sculpt the whole body. They choose a wire-armatured body, so that fine details of character can be expressed through posture and gesture.

Those who do larger clay dolls based on the play concept tend to construct their dolls on soft or minimally wired bodies, similar to the old composition or plastic-limbed "mama doll" commercial toys. But there are no particular rules here.

Sculpted parts assembled on soft cloth body by Marleen Engler. Photo by Meindert Wentzel

My own preference is for a figure that is adjustable while the doll is under construction or packed for shipping but is fixed in display. My experience, therefore, is with constructing dolls having the parts assembled on a wire armature. In some cases, I have combined elements of the solid limb joint—usually at the shoulder to show a low-cut bodice—with the wire armature. How much or how little I might combine these two types depends directly on how I *imagine* the doll will look when completed. In the sculpture stage, then, I have to have at least a rough idea of the final body position and costume.

Sculpted head and breastplate, arms and legs assembled on cloth body by Lilian Tolido-Elzer
Photo by Gerard Elzer

Considering the need for a doll body, we are faced with the fact that we somehow have to get the separate parts together; since we are making a little human figure, the method has to reflect correct human proportion and action. No matter how simple or how complex we might make that construction, it is at all times working as our own skeleton, muscles, and tendons work for us, to hold us up against the forces of gravity.

The tricky part of the doll body in theory and practice is that, whereas our bodies have four separate working actions—bones, muscles, tendons, and joints—the doll body usually does not. All those actions have to be mimicked with one or two materials. The commercial type, where a jointed hard-plastic bone is covered with a soft vinyl skin, is closest to the human body. Artists working with porcelain or wood, where the parts are hollow, are often able to engineer movement by creating systems of springs. One studio artist, Lisa Lichtenfels, creates a wire-and-cloth doll body incorporating all aspects of the human body, although not all parts may actually work. George Stuart constructs a movable armatured body covered with fabric that flawlessly mimics the outward form of a real human. Both of these artists, and others, have developed their methods because the

figure they imagined *required* them to do it that way. Any artists whose doll you respect as a successful art piece will tell you that they work *for* the idea. The doll's concept controls what they do.

Acknowledging the importance of body construction in their dollmaking, four artists provided sketches of the ways they have arrived at solutions to fit their individual concepts. Each follows the basic outline and proportion of the human body but, as you can see, there is infinite variation possible in the actual construction methods and materials.

Elisabeth Flueler-Tomamichel sculpted the heads and hands of *Swiss Bank Gnome* from Sculpey. The sculpted parts were then wired together and a body was modeled over the wire armature from an air-drying product called Helen's Powder™. The second photograph shows *Swiss Bank Gnome* as he was finally costumed. Photos by Christophe Flueler

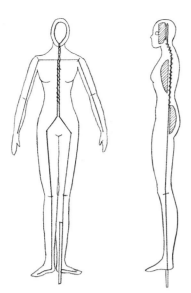

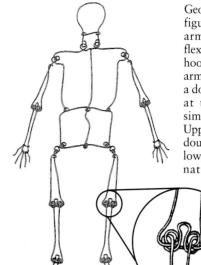

George Stuart constructs his figures over an iron-wire armature which achieves flexibility from a loop and hook system. Lower leg and arm bones are composed of a double run of wire spaced at the joints by a loop simulating the bone end. Upper arm and leg wires are double-looped to attach the lower limbs and to provide natural elbow and knee movement. Limbs are jointed to the torso by creating loops to catch hooks bent in the upper arm and leg wires. Torso stability, spacing, and movement are achieved by a loop grid. The result is a naturally moving skeleton which is then filled in with papier mâché. Mr. Stuart uses best-quality wool felt to create the body skin, and the fatty parts are padded in as necessary with synthetic batting. *Drawing used by permission of Martha Armstrong-Hand*

Sketch of armature wiring made by Carol Nordell. Notice how the wire for the spine curves in an anatomically correct fashion at the neck. Also notice that the major spine wire is straight. The long ends of the head loop wire are twisted around the main spinal wire. Extending the armature wire below the foot allows the doll to be fitted securely into a base without additional support structures that would detract from the final form or look of the character and its costume. Shaded areas are small pieces of ceiling board (plaster wallboard) taped to wires to give interior padding for sculpture. Carol remarks that, although the armatures do move, the movement is only for facilitating sculpture and costuming. Completed figures are permanently posed and not meant to be moved. *Drawing by Carol Nordell*

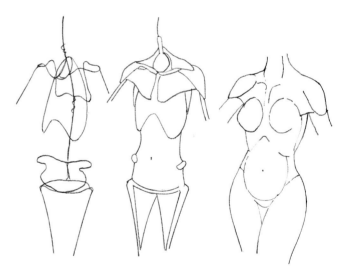

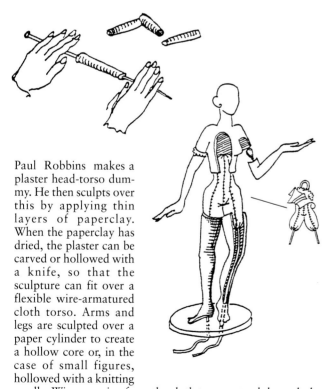

Paul Robbins makes a plaster head-torso dummy. He then sculpts over this by applying thin layers of paperclay. When the paperclay has dried, the plaster can be carved or hollowed with a knife, so that the sculpture can fit over a flexible wire-armatured cloth torso. Arms and legs are sculpted over a paper cylinder to create a hollow core or, in the case of small figures, hollowed with a knitting needle. Wires running from the cloth torso extend through the hollow legs to secure the figure to a solid base. Arms are attached by setting wire loops in the arm top, filling the torso-arm socket with hot-melt glue, and pushing the arm loop into the socket. *Drawing by Paul Robbins*

In assembling most figures made of parts sculpted in hard materials, the soft parts of the fabric or armatured body are usually covered by the costume. Still, proper bone and muscle placement is important to achieve a credible doll. Working with figures with soft-sculpted fabric surfaces led Lisa Lichtenfels to engineer a body which would consistently present the natural look of the skin surface as it reflects the underlying bones and muscles. Lisa creates an armature of bent aluminum sculpture wire which reflects the major bones of the body. Wire bones are wrapped with batting, and padding is added to muscle areas until the body is correctly filled out. A skin sometimes consisting of several layers of two-way stretchable nylon stocking material is then needle-sculpted along the appropriate body contours. Notice that in the areas where bones naturally show directly under the skin, such as collar bones and pelvis, the muscle padding meets but does not cover the bones. *Drawing by Lisa Lichtenfels*

CONSTRUCTION CONSIDERATIONS

No matter what kind of wire you use or how complicated your construction might be, here are three constant considerations in making a wire armature:

1. Provide for correct shoulder and hip width, and for the natural right angle formed by the hang of the arm from the shoulder and the leg from the hip. Imagine two nested three-sided rectangles.

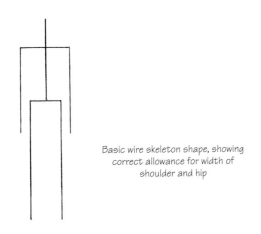

Basic wire skeleton shape, showing correct allowance for width of shoulder and hip

2. The major vertical wiring (spine, legs) must run straight. Bent, spiraled, and wrapped wire create an undesirable spring effect. Wrapping and tucked wire ends will work, but do not use them on any part which will carry weight or need to hold a position.

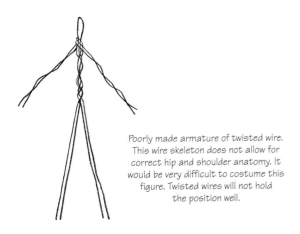

Poorly made armature of twisted wire. This wire skeleton does not allow for correct hip and shoulder anatomy. It would be very difficult to costume this figure. Twisted wires will not hold the position well.

3. The fabric-covered armature must be so bent or needle-sculpted that major joints are properly indicated. Knees and elbows need to be seen as sharply defined as they are on a human body. Nothing is more unsatisfactory than a figure that seems to be composed of limp, jointless limbs. To avoid this, when posing your armature bend the limbs to form *angles* rather than curves. When covering the armature with fabric, be sure to allow elbow and knee angles to show. When costuming the figure, drape or fold the fabric at elbow and knee bends to indicate natural folds of the costume.

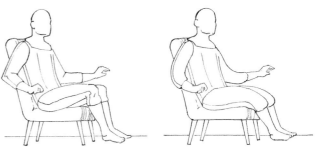

Sharp bends in elbows and knees in this body show natural look.

Lack of elbow and knee definition in this body makes it look boneless.

MATERIALS

During a court appearance as an expert witness, I was asked by an attorney whether I make wire armatures. When I answered in the affirmative, he asked what kind of wire I use. I replied, "Any kind or all kinds." This seemed to startle him; he evidently felt that each artist would use one type of wire. When he asked me to specify wire types, I listed a whole hardware store of types, as well as coat hangers, telephone wire, electrical cable, and sculpture wire. It might have startled him even more to find that an armature can be made of plastic balls hooked together like pop beads.

The most common material for a wire armature is ordinary galvanized wire, available in rolls as hardware supply. For 10" to 20" dolls, 16 gauge is adequate. For larger dolls, you can double the strands of 16-gauge wire. For smaller dolls, use a finer wire, 18 to 20 gauge. For very flexible dolls like a dollhouse type under 10", you can use copper wire; however, for most armatures, I find copper far too soft. Armatures for dolls of any size can be made with an aluminum-alloy wire that artists call "sculpture wire," which is very strong and very flexible, soft enough to bend easily yet strong enough to carry weight. This wire is usually found in art or ceramic supply shops, in several thicknesses. Compared with ordinary galvanized wire or electrical cable, however, it is expensive.

Larger armatures can also be made with electrical cable, found on large spools in hardware electrical departments. You can peel the cable cover off and separate the interior wires for smaller areas, such as finger armatures. In general, most ordinary armatures can be made from 16-gauge wire, but you can use any wire that looks workable and will not rust, including coat hangers.

Warning: Always take care not to bend or twist wires that have been cured inside polymer or paperclay, as you may crack the cured or dried sculpture. When you want to bend your piece to pose it, bend the wires at a point above the hard sculpture. Collectors who own your pieces should also be given this posing caution.

Review: As you sculpted in polymer clay, you have sculpted with a thought to constructing a wire armature and, therefore, arm and leg pieces should have two wires extending out of the cured sculpture. These pieces should also have been scored with a 1/32" to 1/8" groove around the top of each limb, so that a cloth body can be easily attached. If your sculpture was in paperclay, grooves should have been carved; if not, make them before continuing with body construction. If you did not use wires, you will need to drill or cut a tunnel in the material so that you can now set wires in. Depending on the size of the paperclay limb, sometimes you can poke or drill a hole. When the hole is made, insert doubled wire and set with craft glue or wet paperclay. Setting looped wire creates a spring action: each wire presses against the side of the hole, and that pressure helps keep the wires from slipping out.

COVERINGS

For figures 12" and taller, I prefer to use a trouser-weight double-knit fabric. However, as this fabric is no longer popular, I have increasingly been using plain-weave heavyweight muslin or felt. The choice usually depends upon the size and complexity of the body. A larger basic form would be made with felt, a smaller, more detailed form with muslin. If necessary, I will add a skin of stretchy nylon pantyhose fabric or Lycra® and pad it to form specific contours like bust, hip, or elbow.

Bodies under 12" may be made with high-quality stockinette similar to heavy T-shirt weight, or with two-way stretch fabrics like Lycra. Extra care should be taken with the lightweight stretch fabrics to make the form firm. On a body this size, I almost always hand sew all parts.

WEIGHTING, STUFFING, AND PADDING

To wrap the armature types shown, you will need Polyfil Needlepunch® or low-loft quilt batting. You will also need Polyfil stuffing to add padding for contours. A ten-pound bag of ball bearings will make many weight bags. I also use hunters' copper shot. I strongly recommend a weight bag for any doll that is meant to sit, as it adds extra weight to simulate the natural downward force or slump of the body. It also keeps a doll from seeming to float up and off a base or chair. Weighting can help balance a doll in an unusual pose. Most dollmakers will also find it convenient to keep weight materials on hand. You might want to investigate a variety of drapery weights for use in specific areas, or even in parts of the costume. Resist the temptation to make weight bags with organic materials such as rice, beans, or birdseed: they will eventually deteriorate and attract insects. Catbox litter is usable, but does tend to be dusty. Plastic doll-weight pellets are usable but, since they are not as heavy by volume as metal shot, it will take significantly more of them to get the same effect.

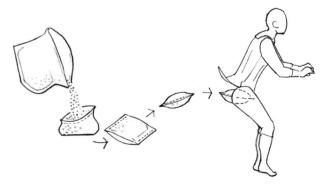

Make a weight bag, tuck it into the body at the back of hip, stitch the body covering to close.

You will also need masking or adhesive tape and wire-cutting pliers.

CONSTRUCTION

The body-covering pieces given in the illustration on the following page are very basic, so enlarge or reduce them as necessary. This body has a rather narrow waist so that costume fabric or gathers will not increase the size or make the piece disproportionate. I find it is usually better to make the body slightly smaller, as it is easier to pad than reduce it. In all cases, at this point, you will have to adjust the body-covering pieces to the type, size, and pose of your figure. Before cutting body pieces, pose your wire armature. Cut pieces and lay them against the body to be sure you allow enough leeway for the action or pose of the doll. For instance, a doll that is bent at the waist will need a little more length in the back of the body. Do *think* about the width of your doll's limbs. Often the size of the foot or the spread of an open hand cannot be put through the width of the machine-stitched fabric cover for the limb. If the hands or feet are too large for the sewn piece to be slipped on, you will need to lay fabric around the limb, turn under the raw edges, pin to hold, and whipstitch the seam by hand. Hand sewing takes only a few minutes more, and it is always much more satisfactory for achieving special details: you can actually needle-sculpt the fabric if necessary.

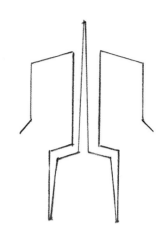

Bend wires at neck, shoulder, and elbow to form arms.
Bend wire at hip to form pelvis and legs.

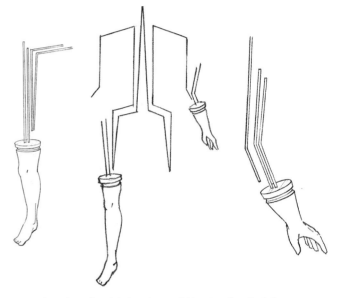

Lay wires of sculpted parts parallel to wires from body form.

Assemble and cover the body as shown:

Wire form for assembling sculpted head, hands, and feet

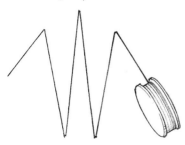

Make a large W with your wire.

Push the W together to form arms and legs.

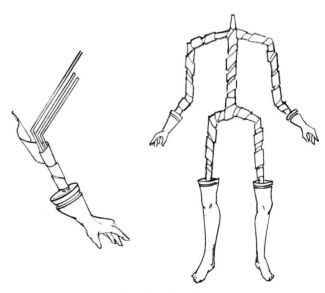

Tape them together.

Wrapped, assembled wire body with strips of quilt batting

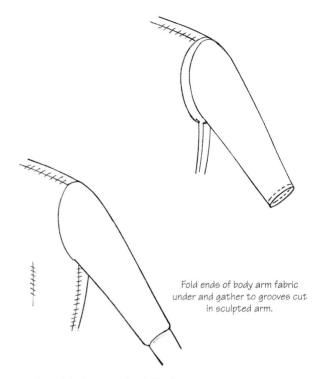

Fold ends of body arm fabric under and gather to grooves cut in sculpted arm.

Hand stitch body seams closed. Needle-sculpt form as necessary to suit your figure's pose and shape.

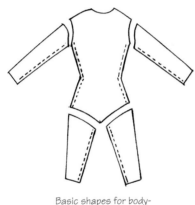

Basic shapes for body-covering pieces. Adjust to fit size and pose of your figure.

Head-on-shoulder plate will be glued or stitched to body fabric.

Head with flange neck. Fold cloth at body neck and, with gathering stitches, sew and tighten to neck groove.

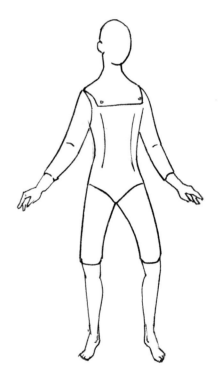

The well-made body should balance, stand, or hold the pose without outside support.

The body cannot be considered complete until you have checked it for a balanced pose and verified that it will *stay* in the pose. A well-made body will stand by itself. Keep trying until it works!

CLOTHING

COSTUME BASICS

If you are attracted—or driven—to make dolls, the two forces involved are usually sculpture and costume. The first involves a love of life and people, and the second involves a love of the theater of life, where we play dress-up in one way or another. For the dollmaker, that love of theater emerges in costuming along with a visual and tactile love affair with color, texture, and form.

If you examine the dolls in this book, you will agree that costume truly makes the doll. It is just as important as the sculpted form and face in bringing the full characterization into being. In the development of the doll's purpose or character, even with the most simple play-doll form, the kind of costume worn is integral to the doll's overall success. Almost without exception, the more well known a doll artist is for good work, the more carefully designed and executed are the costumes. As you become aware of what others do in making their dolls, you will find some creations you do not care for and, on a point-by-point examination, you will probably find that those you do not like have mediocre costuming. Good costuming, like sculpture, requires design and, from the fun standpoint, allows a free hand at experimentation.

For me, the most difficult aspect of dollmaking to talk about is costuming. When I make a costume, I just do it. In sculpture, I can break down the process to a series of small steps. With costuming I can't, because it is a visual process. I change direction at any time, and I break rules at any time—and get away with it. How can I describe a process that works as well breaking the rules as following them? For this chapter, I had to ask myself just what it is that I want you to know about doll costuming. The answer has two parts. First is getting a good grasp of the theory of costume. Second, and just as crucial, is a knowledge of the basic shapes we use in making patterns, and the methods of attaching them to a body.

Let's talk about theory for a while. Even if you start with a goal, when you sculpt, at some point you will be struck with *who* the sculpture is. It will suddenly become clear to you that this head you

are working on is a baby taking its first step, or a clown, or Uncle Fred. At that point, you begin to get a clear image. You think about what that person looks like in more detail as you finish your sculpture. A good artist would probably tell you that he has not only seen the character in the body parts and actions before he finished the sculpture, but that he has also seen the character dressed and in motion. Sometimes, he will admit that the character often takes on life and forces the artist to change his initial visualization. Dolls can be bossy and it is well to listen, because they usually will tell you what is best for them in costuming.

Old Acquaintance by Robert McKinley
A very simple costume accentuates an unusual idea and an interesting pose.
Photo by Robert McKinley

Examine a case of basic but extremely successful costuming. Bob McKinley created a character he called "Old Acquaintance." This was a balding, middle-aged man holding a teddy bear. Right there we have an *idea* that is out of the ordinary, that makes us look twice. You think, "Well, there is nothing exciting about this costume; it's just a shirt, sweater, and trousers." But, you see, that is the point! The artist's use of the everyday costume underscores the uniqueness of the idea. *This* guy with a bear? Bob has made you think about his idea by underlining the ordinariness of the character with a very commonplace costume. When you see the figure, the man looks like any salesman, or banker, or civil servant you have ever seen. But with a bear? If the artist had made an elf with a bear, you might not think twice. You would just accept it as a fantasy.

In addition to the costume Bob used to make his point, he also used the body position. The man is not just holding the bear on his lap or in his arms: he holds the bear out in front of him and looks at it eye-to-eye. You have no doubt that the man is seriously considering this bear. So, the idea is doubly underscored in that the man himself is portrayed as interested in, or maybe surprised by, the idea of the relationship. You get the definite feeling that this is a new emotional experience for the man as well as for you. You share the doll's thoughts and reactions at the moment he is contemplating the relationship. He is just as bemused as you. All of this could not be portrayed in any other way, *or in any other costume.* An artist once said that a good doll was one in which everything that should be done had been done, and done well. Bob's figure should have been costumed simply to make the point, and it was.

A dollmaker is faced with a very different set of choices when he sets out to make a specific character. Portraits of historical figures, known to the audience, must meet or surpass the viewer's expectations. George Stuart, who creates historical figures, accepts the challenge of a specific set of construction problems where choices are extremely limited and must be executed to perfection. Mr. Stuart's figures are meant to take the viewer right into the historical period and, indeed, to make you feel you are in the actual presence of the figure. He must do the portrait sculpture and duplicate the body shape. Even at that point, Captain Cook without his wig, coat, breeches, and sword could be the insurance salesman next door. Costume is integral to the complete projection of the persona. Mr. Stuart does not mess around. The name of his game is authenticity. If he chooses to make a figure in a full suit of armor, he cannot buy one. He must study the history of armor design and construction, find the correct metal, forge a hundred pieces into a hundred different correct shapes, make all the correct fastenings, and then join all the bits so that they move and fall correctly on the body. In short,

Armor constructed for the figure of *Cortes* sculpted and costumed by George Stuart
Photo by Peter d'Aprix

Detail of orphery of *Pope's Cope* by George Stuart. There are no limits to the detail that a costume might require and that an artist might have to create—embroidery, appliqué, couched thread work, and many of the jeweler's arts—to re-create the sumptuousness of this costume. Photo by Peter d'Aprix

he becomes an armorer. If the figures would wear jewels, he becomes a jeweler—modeling, casting, setting stones to replicate the historic design. If the costume requires a specific fabric, he will dye it, paint it, embroider it as necessary—and it wouldn't surprise me to learn that he has actually woven needed cloth.

So, how do you know what your problems and choices are? Basically, it is a matter of observation. Either you become very good at visualizing your character—running a film of him in your head and observing all the details, actively looking for those details in your mental picture—or you observe your fellow humans in everyday situations.

For instance, your sculpture suggests an elderly man you call "Uncle Fred." Tomorrow, you are at the supermarket in line behind an elderly man. You note that he walks with a stoop and a shuffle; he is thin, and his well-worn clothes are not tight and tucked; his sweater pulls up in the center back because his shoulders have rounded from his stoop. You note that his shirt front pops out at his little tummy bulge, and he has no one to sew on buttons anymore. His shirt is buttoned at the neck, and he wears an old-fashioned tie, trying to maintain dignity and decorum. You note that his pant cuffs are a bit frayed from dragging the ground because of his posture, and his shoes are worn from his shuffle. All these observations become part of what you must put into the costume.

Don't forget that Uncle Fred's costume should include accessories. If you depict Uncle Fred's shopping cart with candy, colored dry breakfast cereal, hot dogs and buns, and a troll doll, it would seem Uncle Fred was not shopping for himself. Maybe he was shopping for a visit from his grandchildren. On the other hand, you could show Uncle Fred with a cart full of organic foods: we would know instantly that he had read all the labels to care for his age and health. If you show Uncle Fred with all those organic foods in his cart reaching for a big bag of potato chips, what story would that tell?

Now your problem is to assemble fabrics and fibers and leather and other materials to give the *illusion* of the materials you see in your visualization, to create a unified costume that reflects all your observations about the old man who becomes Uncle Fred. You begin to think analytically and with all your experiences of fiber.

You must now hold three elements in the forefront of your mind: scale, scale, and scale! Scale has to do with the correct size and proportion of materials, including weights, textures, and colors. Usually, in design, color and texture and weight would be considered as separate from scale, but in costuming they all must interrelate and work under the umbrella of scale. The problem for the costumer is that manufacturers make fabrics for real humans. All fabric is proportioned to human scale. It becomes our job to learn how to deceive the viewer into believing that human-scale fabric is really something made by elves to fit dolls! The artist who can pull off this illusion is a real Houdini of dollmakers.

In the case of Uncle Fred's sweater, you know that the texture and the drape of the fabric are going to be very important. You know that human-scale knit fabric like the real old man's sweater will be far too large in scale. You also know that most small-scale sweater knits do not come in masculine or sporty patterns. What to do? You might consider combing the women's T-shirt rack in a thrift store for a possible small-scale substitute. You might think of other sorts of knit garments. I have used argyle socks to re-create small-scale sporty sweaters. You might even have to find thin yarns and thread, and knit a sweater yourself. Oddly, many dollmakers do not consider that sometimes the fabric they are trying to re-create is available on the actual human-sized garment. For instance, men's suiting and men's shirting fabrics are often very finely textured wools and cottons. Pinpoint shirt stripes in human scale look a bit large but are usable on a doll. As long as you are careful to avoid large seams and bulky facings, these fabrics can work quite well. How would you re-create an old pair of scuffed shoes? New real and fake leathers are readily available. Old leather could come from very worn gloves. Materials can be distressed by bleaching, fading, tea-dying, even singeing and rubbing ashes or powdered chalks into them. Think how ineffectual a hobo character is going to be in a crispy new suit.

Working very closely with scale is *fit*. No matter how well the fabrics and colors are chosen, the costume must look as if it belongs on the body. It needs to move with the body and to drape correctly. When the sweater is put on, it must be draped in order to hang over the tummy in the front and, in the case of Uncle Fred, pull up in the back. There must be wrinkles where the elbow bends, and there must be a point to indicate the elbow bone. If the figure is going to be seated, the bone of the knee must be indicated under the fabric. Recently, I saw a doll reportedly sold at a very high price. The doll was well made in general; however, it was a seated man, with legs bent, in trousers, who had no visible knee caps. The illusion was not of leg under trousers but of bent rubber tube. That irregularity caused an otherwise carefully worked piece to fail to convey its illusion. Never forget fit! If the body is turning, make sure the fabric pulls to show the tension. As I write this, I am wearing a sweatshirt covered by a quilted flannel shirt. With all that bulk, when my arm is bent in a 45° angle to type, there are <u>five</u> wrinkles in the shirt fabric at the inside elbow bend and a discernible elbow bone on the outside. A bulky costume does *not* mean a shapeless one.

Three points about color: One factor to remember when selecting colors for your doll is that doll's complexion. Like a human, the flesh color (paint or natural clay) will determine what colors look best on the doll. Don't allow yourself to be committed to yellow if the doll looks drab or feverish in that color. Do not stereotype. Some fair-skinned people look very good in hot, bright colors, and not all brown skin tones look good in olive and orange. Use what the doll needs. Second, remember that color is scaled in brightness. Bright and high-intensity colors can overwhelm some dolls. Suppose you want a truly bright robin's-egg blue. On a human, you can use the real color. On a doll, in order to get the illusion of bright, you might have to tone down one or two shades. Toning down will not subdue; it will bring the brightness to scale for the doll's size. Third, if you are selling your work, your buyers will have very specific color tastes of their own. Not all people will be able to verbalize their color opinions, either. They will just say, "I don't like that doll." It might not be the doll; it could be the colors on the doll. For instance, to one person the rose colors will be lovely, while to another they will be drab and soggy. If you are planning to show a group of dolls for sale, it is a good idea to have samples in several color schemes.

If you take a close look at the clothing people put on dolls, you will see that, no matter how complex a costume might appear, it really boils down to variations on the basic shirt or basic trousers. With few exceptions, all our clothing derives from the form of the simple flat piece of woven goods or the animal skin. What impresses the viewer about the costume on a doll is the originality of the variation and embellishment of the basic forms, and how well they co-ordinate with the character and finish of the doll.

When you are making doll costumes, remember first to make the viewer *think* the costume is the same as a human costume, but it does not have to be an exact duplication. You have lots of liberty to fake and fudge in order to create the *impression* of the character. Additionally, you want the viewer to react to the character first ("What a darling baby!") and the costume second ("My, what a charming and nicely embroidered dress!"). You never want the viewer to react first to the costume materials or shape. You never want the viewer to think, "Wow, those buttons are too big, and that seam is too bulky."

Margaret Finch allowed the draping of soft pastel fabrics to accentuate the character of *Persephone*, sculpted by her daughter, Marta Finch-Kozlosky. Photo by Charles Kozlosky

People who are drawn to dollmaking usually have a fascination with costume as well as character, and many already have experience with sewing their own clothes. The same principles of cutting, shaping, and draping are involved. In making doll clothes, you need to remember that *weight* of fabric and *size* or scale of pattern are extremely important to a successful statement of character.

In considering scale of fabric prints, again, you must remember that the doll is going to require a miniaturized pattern. A small-scale floral print from a human dress might look like dinner plates on a doll's dress. A fabric with a ¼" stripe will be the equivalent of a 12" stripe, much bigger than any real person would wear. A trick for determining scale in fabrics is to lay your doll on a piece of heavy paper and trace its outline. Then draw the general shape of the costume part over the doll's outline and cut it out for a template.

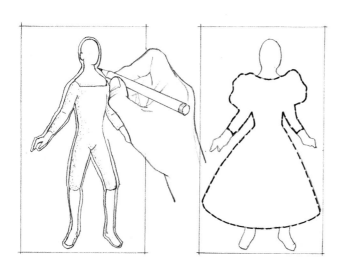

Take your template to your fabric boxes or to the fabric shop and test sizes by laying it over several patterns. The template will give you a rough but good idea of what the print will look like as a finished costume part. Every one of us has found some lovely bit of fabric or trim and jealously saved it for that one special doll. The day comes when you finally have that doll, and it is ready to dress. You get that piece of fabric and you start to work out the costume design. Oops, it will not work. It is too large or the wrong color. You try to use it several different ways, none of which looks right. What to do? Reject it! Put it away and save it for another day.

This costume of *Odile-Odette LaTourette,* by Susanna Oroyan, is purposely constructed of dark, rich colors, textures, and prints with embellishments of fur, tassels, ostrich plumes, and jewels to create a feeling of old New Orleans mystery. Photo by W. Donald Smith

In costuming, I find that often the doll will tell you what it wants or needs. You just have to learn to hear that tiny voice. When you put three different potential dress fabrics up against the doll, you are not making the decision: the elements of the doll—its type, skin tone, size, and character—will direct you to make the right choice, if you listen. There have been times when I thought I knew exactly what the doll needed. Once I had decided to create a heavy, ornate costume from brocade. I worked and I worked, I built and I re-built; no matter what I did, it just would not hang right or look right. I finally shoved the doll in the corner with her face to the wall. Three months later, I happened to throw some tulle on the desk and voilà! It was tulle she wanted. She needed yards and yards of fluffy, ruffly skirts, not heavy brocade. It just took me some time to hear the little voice. You need to be ready to experiment and to change your mind in the middle of the process.

So, your doll is all made, painted, and assembled on a body, but there are no patterns available for the costume you envision. What to do? If your doll is a play doll or soft-bodied type, you might be able to shortcut the design phase by using doll clothes patterns from major pattern manufacturers. These patterns are usually available to fit standard soft or vinyl-bodied dolls 8" to 24" tall. They also will provide the basic forms for skirts, bodices, blouses, jackets, and dresses for baby, toddler, and child dolls. Your local craft shop will also carry several pattern books. If you are going to use commercial patterns, before sewing cut the patterns out and check the fit to the body. Adjust where necessary.

If your figures are to be character types or will have complex costuming, you will need to make your own patterns by adapting the basic forms to the body you have constructed. If you have experience in sewing clothing and if you are making a doll where the costume is not meant to be taken off, then you can make an appliquéd costume. In this approach, only major seams (skirt, bodice side seams, sleeves) are machine sewn. The pieces are pinned to the body to make a close fit, edges are lapped and pinned, and all finish sewing is done by hand. This eliminates bulky seams and allows the costume to be fitted to the action of the body. When a costume is constructed this way, the folds of the fabric can be adjusted to fall naturally with the position of the doll and can be stitched into permanent position. This method also allows more fitted styles when the fixed body position would not allow a pre-constructed jacket or bodice to be put on.

Fitting the commercial pattern or creating your own is a matter of what the fashion industry calls *draping*. At this point, your doll becomes a dress form. The paper pattern or throw-away fabric is pinned on the body, pleats or darts are taken to make the fabric fit the curvatures of the body, and pattern material outside the seam lines is trimmed away, forming a basic pattern. That basic shape is then traced and enlarged by a uniform amount to create a seam allowance. If the basic pattern is re-traced on muslin, you can sew it up to make a sample for checking the fit. A muslin test sample, or toile, will allow you to be sure of the pattern size before cutting into your good fabric. You can see step-by-step pictures of this process in Robert McKinley's book *Dollmaking: One Artist's Approach.*

Any serious doll costumer should build a library of fashion reference books for specific details of historical styles. In general, all doll costumes except abstract and fantasy types will be constructed ex-

actly like human clothing with one important consideration: eliminate bulk!

To examine the actual process of constructing doll costumes, let's take a step-by-step journey through the dressing of my Mulliner Family figures "Archie" and "Cousin Millie," because together they incorporate most of the basic pattern forms.

Archie the Architect by Susanna Oroyan is a simple fellow whose clothes were designed to portray the everyday wear—shirt coming un-tucked, tie askew—of a man at work in an office. Photo by W. Donald Smith

I visualized Archie as a middle-aged architect in his office. (He now does, in fact, "work" every day at the corner of my husband's drafting table.) This meant casual shoes, plain trousers, shirt, and sweater in contemporary textures and rather unexciting colors. The first challenge, then, is picking colors and textures that would make an appropriate impact without hitting the viewer in the teeth. Instead of plain brown leather for shoes, I used old pigskin gloves and incorporated the overcast-stitched seams into tasseled penny loafers. I would have liked denim for the trousers, but it is too heavy and difficult to detail in scale for an 18" figure, so I compromised with a very thin pinwale corduroy. Shirts are shirts, and this one was a plain white cotton. I examined many sweater knits and, finally, I used the wrong side of one pattern in combination with a co-ordinating piece of ribbed knit for the cuffs.

Since the feet were sculpted to stand flat, I knew that it would be difficult to pull narrow-legged trousers over shoes, so the trousers were cut and sewn before the shoes were put on. First I cut the basic shape for the two major pattern pieces.

Typical Trouser Construction

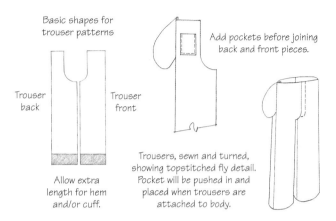

Basic shapes for trouser patterns

Trouser back

Trouser front

Allow extra length for hem and/or cuff.

Add pockets before joining back and front pieces.

Trousers, sewn and turned, showing topstitched fly detail. Pocket will be pushed in and placed when trousers are attached to body.

The back piece was cut with a greater curve, to accommodate the curve of the buttocks (and the body weight bag that allows him to perch on the edge of the stool). Both pieces were cut 2" longer than the leg measurement, to allow for take-up of the bend at knee and hip and a turned-back cuff. Then, I sewed on the back patch pockets, as it is always easier to sew detail on flat pieces. I also sewed pocket pieces onto the sides of each back and front piece.

With right sides together, I joined each front piece to each back piece at the side seam, including the pocket. The trousers were turned and a fly front was detailed by topstitching the outline. The trousers were slipped onto the body and pinned into place, and the pockets were pushed in.

At this point, the costume began to be fitted with specific attention to making it accentuate the position of the body. That means leg bend folds were pinned into place and the exact line of the waist pinned.

Now, I pulled the trouser legs up as far as I could and pinned them in place so I could add socks and shoes. Shoes are a messy business and require the figure to stand on its head while being shod, so I usually try to get them on before the majority of the costuming. Stockings in this case are simple white T-shirt fabric tubes. Fold a length of fabric, and stitch to create a back seam. When

turned and pulled on, the tube naturally creases at the ankle. Socks go only to the side of the foot, to eliminate the bulk of a seam and extra fabric at the shoe sole. Secure the stocking bottom by stitching in a crisscross fashion across the bottom of the foot, pulling 1/8" of the raw edge over the edge of the foot. (If I had been making a woman's sheer stocking, I would have measured fabric exactly to the width of the leg at the ankle, pinned edges together, and hand sewn a whipstitched seam.)

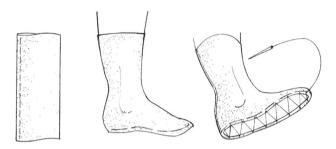

Here is how generic shoes are made: A good doll shoe is made in the same way as human shoes. You must learn a bit about the art of cobbling. A shoe is constructed over a last, or model of the shape. The last does not conform to the shape of a real foot unless the shoe is to be custom-made or orthopedic. The shoe consists of an upper, a sole, and a heel. Uppers are best made of soft leather or vinyl. Ultrasuede® and fine kidskin are especially nice, and some fabrics can also be used. An inner sole of cardboard will need to be inserted if the shoe is to be removable.

It is not necessary to cut the upper to a pattern before beginning. Simply cut a rectangular piece about 1/2" longer and 1/2" wider than the foot imprint. Make a cut into one end 1/4" longer than the width of the ankle.

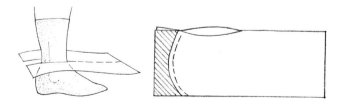

Fold the piece lengthwise and machine stitch at the cut end to create a curved seam at the back of the heel. Turn the piece right side out and pull over the foot. You might have to enlarge the cut slightly to pull the material over the foot. With one hand, form the shoe material tightly around the foot and trim so that ⅛" of material extends beyond the edge of the bottom of the foot. Hold the foot upside down, sole facing up.

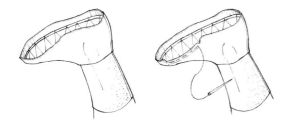

With a double-threaded needle, run a gathering stitch around the shoe fabric along the edge of the foot. Gather the material to the foot. Clip excess material from the gathers. With the double-threaded needle and starting at the instep, sew crisscross, catching the fabric from side to side around the toe and heel. Stitch back and forth until the fabric lies flat against the foot. Turn the foot and make sure the upper material lies flat against the foot in a smooth fit. The shoe upper is now formed.

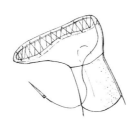

Place the foot over cardboard or leather (I used cork for Archie's and Millie's soles) and trace around it to make the shoe sole and heel pieces.

Cut out and glue to the sole of the foot over crossed stitching. In order to hold the sole firmly against the foot, you can wrap threads around the foot until the glue dries. Clean up any glue runs as you see them. Note that leather glued to leather bonds quickly and very firmly.

Finishing the upper: If the shoe will have a low-cut vamp, use small, sharply pointed scissors to snip away material to the desired shape. Finishing details such as heels, high tops, lacings, ties, and straps are glued or stitched on.

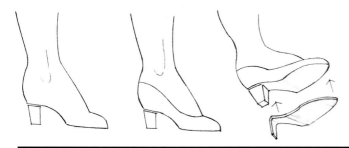

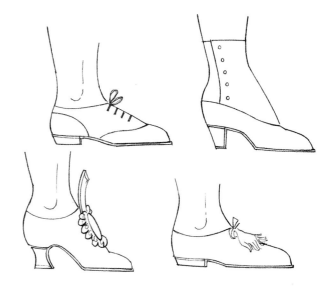

Fabric for Archie's shirt was laid against his body and cut in the basic pattern, with extra width at the tail to allow for his tummy—not a lot, because I wanted to indicate that his shirt was just a little tight with a modicum of button strain! After checking that the front piece fit, I cut, positioned, and sewed the pocket on. Button holes were positioned and created by sewing a small, tight line of machine zigzag stitches. Side seams were machine sewn and the shirt body slipped on. I cut the sleeves somewhat narrow, because I did not want too much bulk under the sweater; then I sewed the seams and pulled it up to the shoulder. The sleeve tops were eased by hand gathering, the ends turned under and stitched with an appliqué stitch to the shoulders. I eased the cuff end to the wrist with hand gathering stitches. Cuffs and collar were cut and machine sewn *separately*. Remember the two rules: It only has to *look* like a cuff or collar, and we always want to eliminate seam bulk. Furthermore, no one in her right mind wants to machine sew a faced collar attachment with a 1" radius! I pinned the cuffs and stitched to secure them. Then I pinned the collar over the raw edge of the shirt neck and stitched the front button point. An additional line of glue was run along the collar-neck join to prevent slippage. Buttons were positioned and sewn on. I made a tie by folding a lightweight striped silk on the bias, sewing, turning, and pressing until I had the desired length and shape. The bias strip was then knotted at one end and tacked to the shirt front, the collar turned over the tie and sewn with a tack stitch to create the illusion of a collar bar. The following illustrations show a generic man's shirt and tie.

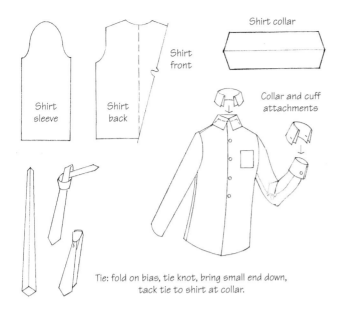

Shirt collar

Shirt front

Shirt sleeve

Shirt back

Collar and cuff attachments

Tie: fold on bias, tie knot, bring small end down, tack tie to shirt at collar.

With Archie placed on his stool, and working with the final pose in mind, I tucked the shirt and pinned it into the top of the trousers to simulate a bit of sloppiness. Then, I folded a band of trouser fabric and laid it over the top of the trousers to form a waistband. The waistband was hand stitched into place with the ends overlapped. I cut a leather belt and made a buckle. The belt was pinned over the top of the waistband. Belt loops were sewn and glued around the belt. The whole unit was then glued onto the trousers over the waistband, corrected as necessary to preserve the exactly pull of the tummy against the belt.

I cut Archie's sweater with a raglan sleeve to reduce bulk, machine sewed and attached it in the same way as the shirt. In order to vary texture and color, I used the wrong side of the knit to make a front inset. Here is another sweater:

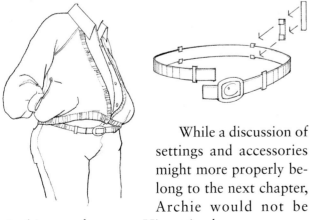

While a discussion of settings and accessories might more properly belong to the next chapter, Archie would not be Archie out of context. His setting became a group project and his environment so real that he has become a destination point for office visitors: he receives mail and occasionally gifts from traveling partners. His eye shade was made from a green Mylar® report cover. We reduced my husband's colored renderings, real project drawings, and specification books, certificates, and diplomas (many times!) with a photocopier. Archie also has a calculator (simulated by a calculator wristwatch face), electric eraser, clamp-on pencil sharpener, sliding parallel bar, and assorted drafting tools.

Cousin Millie by Susanna Oroyan
Photo by W. Donald Smith

Cousin Millie's costume, although a dress, was constructed almost exactly along the same steps as Archie's shirt. The major difference is that pin tucks were stitched into the fabric before the bodice was cut, and pressed pleats were set into the skirt to ease the fabric to the waist. "Little person believability" was established by the 1/16" windowpane featherweight pure silk dress fabric, and the pose. Notice that, although Millie appears to be sitting still, there is real body tension throughout the piece. Her leg is turned to show bracing, the shoulder of the arm holding the cup is lower, and both hands are holding something. Her skirt is a little out of place from having just crossed her legs, and she is just about to take a sip of tea. The following illustrations show a generic woman's blouse front.

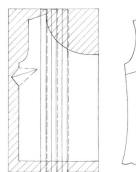

Dart for shaping bust

Pleat fabric before cutting pattern.

lowance to less than ⅛" from the seam. Press the seam. Turn the fabric so the right side is inside, and press so that the seam line forms a sharp edge. Sew the second seam ⅛" from the folded sewn edge. Turn right sides out again.

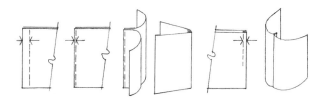

Authenticity: In order to re-create the feel of historical costume, you need to make the correct underpinnings. This means making panniers for an eighteenth-century dress to fall correctly. This means creating hoop skirts for the Civil War era, and bustles and bustle pads for the later years. Did you know that the bustle back was as much created by the wire form as by an elaborate system of inside gathering tapes? Did you know that costumes which look to be one-piece dresses in the historical portraits and drawings are often three-piece costumes consisting of a chemise, a corset, and a skirt? Almost every age, including ours, has modified clothing to achieve shaping not natural to the human body. It means that, for the Edwardian look, one might actually have to construct the body with an S curve. Study the tailoring gimmicks used in the various eras. Learn to re-construct them if you want your historical figures to look realistic.

Even the small accessories count in this delicately detailed purse created by Margaret Finch for the figure of *Cinderella*. Photo by Charles Kozlosky

ADDITIONAL COSTUMING NOTES

Panties and pantalettes: These garments are variations on the basic trouser pattern. Adjust the leg width as desired. On very small legs, you will find it easier to sew lace or trim bands on before sewing the side seams.

French seams: Two seams are made so that raw fabric edges are enclosed. On any garment, this is a nice finishing touch, as people find the urge to see what's underneath irresistible. To make a French seam, sew pieces together along the sewing line with right side *out*. Cut away seam al-

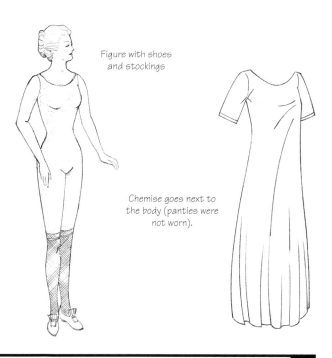

Figure with shoes and stockings

Chemise goes next to the body (panties were not worn).

A vest-type corset is laced on over the chemise. Panniers, made of reeds, were tied on at waist to extend the skirts.

A decorative petticoat was tied on over the pannier. A stomacher made of quilted or stiffened fabric was pinned in place over the corset front. Separate pockets were tied around the waist over the petticoat.

The dress, open at the front, was pinned and tied on over the stomacher. Slits in the side of the dress skirt allowed access to the separate pocket hanging underneath.

Gathering tapes on the inside of the dress skirt could be pulled and tied to form a puffed look. In casual wear, petticoats were sometimes pulled up through the pocket openings in the dress to allow freedom of movement.

WIGGING

The most important fact to remember about doll hair is that a little bit goes a very long way. Human hair is an almost microscopic bit of thready material. If a human hair, fine as it is, fits a human head in scale, how thin does it have to be in scale on a doll? Right, at least three times smaller! That will be impossible. Therefore, what you need to remember is that human hair is likely to be too large for most dolls. For realism, you will need to work with mohair or acrylic roving. For larger dolls, a doll wig of human or synthetic hair will work if you can find a style you like that is *not* bulky. Unfortunately, in order to use a commercial wig, many dollmakers find they have to take it apart and reduce the bulk. Other makers have taken human wigs and simply cut them down or stripped off the wefted hair strips and re-sewn them onto a smaller cap.

Some dollmakers enjoy creating wigs. This can be done by wefting the chosen fiber. Wefting is essentially attaching hair to a band by weaving or sewing. The easiest way to weft is to lay hair material in a piece of tissue paper, machine a zigzag stitch, and peel off the paper after stitching. Wefted lengths can then be glued onto the head or onto a cap made of a thin stretch material.

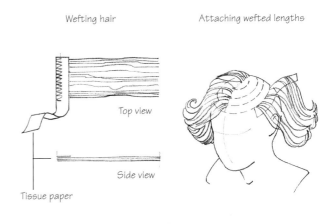

Wefting hair

Top view

Side view

Tissue paper

Attaching wefted lengths

Others prefer to eliminate the bulk of weft stitching by weaving or tying bunches of hair through an open-weave fabric or netting, much as a rug is hooked.

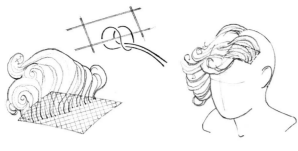

Woven or tied wigging   Applying woven wigging

Attaching hair by gluing into sculpted part line groove

Hair may also be implanted into a coat of glue or liquid latex painted on the skull, or it may be implanted by coating the head with wax and using a hot needle to insert hair strands in small plugs.

For babies or toddlers with thin, fine hair, a hole can be carved in the center crown area and a small bundle of hair glued in and smoothed around the head.

Implanting hair

Attaching hair by gluing into center crown hole

If you use fabric, fur, or animal hide with hair still attached, it looks more natural if the skull is carved or sculpted lower in the area to be wigged. This allows the hide to sit lower than the hair line, so that it appears that skull and scalp are continuous. No hide line shows above the surface.

Applying hide wigging

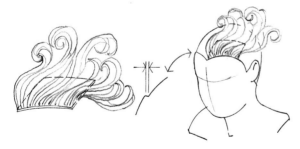

Skull has been sculpted approximately 1/32" lower to allow hide to sit flush with skull when applied.

If you use unwefted mohair, a part line can be made to look natural by carving a groove in the skull, running glue along it, and pressing the hair down into it. This makes it appear that the hair has the natural lift it would have along a part line.

One of the most difficult aspects of costuming is working successfully to portray a free-flowing kimono. *Turandot* by Carol Nordell shows how the artist carefully must combine fabric weight, pattern scale, and draping to achieve the necessary graceful and free-flowing look. Photo by Tony Gezirjian

ACCESSORIES, DISPLAY, & FUN STUFF

ACCESSORIES

Some of the most fun in dollmaking comes in creating the final assembly and finishing touches for display. This is where we really get to play with our dolls, even for just a little while.

When we accessorize our dolls they finally can come to life. The space they occupy, the furnishings they use, and the objects they hold—all place the character in an identifiable, life-like environment. Almost every doll can use some extra touch, if only a painted base or a single flower in its hand. In the end, dolls are little people, and even little people will look better if connected just a bit to their own worlds. Thoughtful construction of settings, displays, and accessories makes the difference between "Ho hum, just another doll" and "My, *what* a doll!" If a doll is worth making, it is worth completing as well as we can through the finishing touches.

Most dollmakers don't need to be told much about accessories and display, which are already a part of the initial vision of the doll. Dollmakers are really *illustrators* as much as sculptors or costumers. Many of our doll ideas come from free associations with objects we find interesting in our environment. Many are a result of wanting to re-tell a familiar story with figures we create.

Accessorizing is truly the game of scale played once more. What a tricky, challenging game it can be! If you make miniature or dollhouse figures, where one inch equals twelve human inches, accessories to scale are easy to find. Craft shops and miniature suppliers have small-scale examples of almost any item. However, most of us make dolls to fit the scale of the head sculpture. If we find an item to fit our figure, it is usually a happy accident. In most cases, everything we add to that doll must be made or assembled by hand to fit the particular scale. Most dollmakers will admit that, in addition to boxes of fabric and trims, they also have bags of little found objects just waiting for the right doll. Anything that looks remotely usable will be stored away. Why else would I have three ornamental sword-shaped paper knives, a box full of plastic bottle tops, a major selection of

toy Christmas ornaments, and an assortment of key rings made with little leather purses and sporting equipment?

Sometimes, a perfectly charming small object will still not match a doll's form and expression. Take the case of the "Photographer." There are working miniature cameras with realistic detail. However, in the case of my photographer, this kind of camera looked "too real." My figure was a character, and he needed a character camera. So, I had to make one. I put together a wood block, a metal insert from a ballpoint pen, dowel sticks, and brass jewelry findings, to make an old-fashioned box camera on a tripod. Its simple, almost abstract look worked better with the doll's cartoon features. Of course, the camera suggested "Watch the birdie," and this meant finding just the right kind of abstract bird. Realistic birds at the craft shop were considered, but the winner was a little eraser bird from a pencil.

Photographer by Susanna Oroyan
20", Sculpey
Photo by W. Donald Smith

There is an unfortunate tendency for people to spend a great deal of time and serious concentration on creating a well-sculpted, well-designed doll made to human scale and then stick on a found object in human scale. Jewelry and buttons are often so used, and the effect can so shock the sensibilities that any positive impact is lost. On the other hand, sometimes an out-of-scale object can be used with great effect if the impression is *meant to be* unusual. In the case of the figure I call "The 8th Empress," the human-scale pocket watch works because the figure is obviously fantastical: we can therefore accept the disproportion. The fantastical object is also the only accessory in the composition, so our attention is focused on it and we ask, "What does this mean?" Because this is fantasy, we have more imaginative freedom.

The 8th Empress by Susanna Oroyan
20", Sculpey
Photo by W. Donald Smith

In the case of a figure representing a more realistic human, such as a grandmother in a rocking chair, the real-world association gives us a pretty specific set of check points. We know that the old woman's dress would not have buttons as large as saucers. When a costume has real-world shirt buttons, either they are obviously meant to be odd or the doll is poorly scaled. Similarly, our expectations would be jolted to see her wearing a cameo pin one-third the size of her head.

The ultimate in play dolls is the soft-bodied, boneless type. This doll is made so that the recipient, usually a child, does the interacting and the accessorizing. She gets to prop and make pretend poses, and to find objects for the doll to play with. This doesn't mean that the maker can't give the child a little boost: you can provide chair, bed, toys, tea sets, or trousseau.

Usually we think of finding accessories to go with the doll, but how about making a doll to go with the objects? Suppose you are like me and have collected a number of small teddy bears over the years. Why not make a doll who collects teddy bears? Everyone should have a Santa doll or Christmas figure that can provide an excuse for *your* collection of small Christmas ornaments and novelties. If your passion is costuming, why not create a doll with a wardrobe? There's an excuse for using treasured bits of lace, beaded trims, and special fabrics. Peddler dolls, male and female, are also types where accessories can become a reason for being.

DISPLAY STANDS AND BASES

The play or interactive doll usually does not have a stand, but almost every other kind has some sort of stand, seat, or back prop. Least interesting, and least likely to accentuate the character or the design, is a plain commercial metal stand. The metal stand is made to hold manufactured collectible dolls. When it is used with artistic figures, the upright support conflicts with the legs, and the waist grips create awkward bulges under coats or skirts, destroying the line of the costume. Frequently, the stand will lift the doll so that its feet are suspended in mid-air. If you can give thought to making the doll, you can give thought to its most effective presentation. If you make a doll that will work with the waist support of a metal stand, use it, but decorate it to accentuate the doll. For instance, if you have an elf or fairy, cover the metal upright with fabric and over that work woodland flowers, twigs, and dried materials.

For a straight standing figure, you can create a simple base from scrap wood or découpage blocks from your craft supplier. These can be sanded, stained, painted, or covered with co-ordinating fabric, then drilled for a hollow metal upright. Hollow metal rods of various sizes are available at hobby shops specializing in findings for model enthusiasts. A wire around the waist can fit down inside the metal upright rod as with the commercial metal stands. Alternatively, if you consider the base when you sculpt the figure, you can provide a hole in the sole of each foot. These holes can take a small rod or coat-hanger wire to peg the doll into the base. Either base allows the doll to be taken off for packing or storing. Of course, you can add a flower or a few leaves and stones, or cover the base to simulate floor covering.

Not all dollmakers are woodworkers, but all dollmakers should have a small saw and drill. Objects to create display bases can be found at thrift shops, garage sales, and flea markets. Almost anything works: I have used inverted salad bowls, cheese boards, chopping blocks, candle holders, plastic boxes, and lazy Susan bases.

Doll furniture, especially a variety of chairs, is readily available. Most craft suppliers carry at least one or two types. Basket markets carry examples in wicker, bentwood, and reed. These ready-made furnishings are usually scaled to the play doll. Many, however, can be used for the human-scaled figure, if you select carefully. You can also have fun trimming and upholstering these pieces to co-ordinate with your doll's costume.

SETTINGS

Creating vignettes is also another way to accessorize and accentuate the character of a doll. Carefully chosen settings and accessories can make a portrait figure. In all my dollmaking, I have made only three portrait figures—intentionally! In the first case, the woman commissioning the piece specifically provoked my imagination: she refused to send me a picture of her husband, the man I was to portray. I created a figure from her verbal description and, in doing so, was careful to include such details as scuffed and untied shoes, lollipops and cigars in his pocket, and an electrician's tool belt. Even though I had never seen so much as a photo of Alex, his family

agreed instantly that I had captured him, and all because of the appropriate accessories.

Mike by Susanna Oroyan. 17", Super Sculpey
Photo by W. Donald Smith

Accessories and settings were also important in the portraits of Betty and Mike. Betty commissioned a portrait of her friend Mike for his fortieth birthday; she supplied me with photos and written details. She knew that the figure would be a character, merely suggestive of his real looks. For my portrait of Mike, an avid spare-time gardener, I placed him on a rustic bentwood bench and sculpted a Celluclay brick path over a wood base. With Mike on the bench were small garden tools, fishing rod, and backpack. I made seedling trays from sections of a plastic candy-box liner. Garden tools were made by extending handles on dollhouse spade and rake. As a medical professional, the real Mike carries a telephone pager: I re-created this from an inexpensive digital watch. Items in his backpack, such as medical equipment, coins, and a tiny elf, all created the illusion of "Mike-ness." Later, Mike commissioned a figure of Betty to accompany his figure on the bench. Betty, a nurse and doll collector, was shown with miniature dolls and a first-aid kit—and holding a large diamond ring, since Mike was using the "Betty" doll as a prop to pop the question! Creating settings and accessories for your dolls can be a delightful challenge.

Betty by Susanna Oroyan. 15", Super Sculpey
Photo by W. Donald Smith

FUN STUFF

Eventually, a dollmaker will use the clays to make something *else*. At first, it will be a different dollmaking application or a specific accessory. A cloth dollmaker may use polymer or paper-based clay for a sculpted face form to be covered with fabric. Once you start, however, there is no end: follow your creative paths.

Masks: The doll wearing or holding a mask allows the maker to portray multiple characters or personalities in one figure. Masks for dolls are usually made from molds taken from the original head. You need reproduce only the front third or half of the head. Clay material is simply pushed in and pulled out, but it helps if you dust the inside of the mold with talcum to ensure a smooth release. The mask may be hollowed out carefully before cooking, or trimmed with a sharp tool when hard. If the mask is to be used as the actual face, attached to a cloth doll head, it may be glued right to the cloth. If it is to be sewn on, don't forget to punch sewing holes at attachment points before curing. A mask to be sewn on should be as thin as the material will allow, as sewing into a cloth head through deep holes can be awkward.

Buttons and button covers: Sewing accessory suppliers stock detachable button covers. Small doll heads can be attached to the covers, and the entire button cover can be removed from the clothing for laundering.

Jewelry: This is where the dollmaker can *really* have fun with sculpted forms. You can make free-hand original sculptures, or make molds. Pins, pendants, and earrings seem obvious, but what about bracelets and belt buckles? A word of caution: earrings should not be made to be too heavy, but bracelets and buckles that might be subject to tension should be made with more thickness of clay.

Mug dwellers and pot people: These are a special breed of doll people developed by artist Maureen Carlson—a nifty way to make your plants happy or to put a smile on your face with the wake-up cup of coffee.

Game pieces: The idea of creating thirty-two different figures for the ultimate chess set might be a little staggering, but you could start by making sculpted doll game pieces for board games.

Christmas ornaments: Make a Nativity crèche, of course, and everything from tree-top angels to elves, fairies, snowmen, and Santas.

Dolls on lampshades, shade pulls, doorstops....

Linda Gill made *Molly Ann—A Finder's Keeper* with body parts sculpted in bread dough and assembled on a cloth body. The figure is supported by wooden dowels which extend from the body through the Super Sculpey shoes and into a wood base. Photo by Hoppe Photography

Lilian Tolido sculpted a fantasy in Paperclay for her complete vision of *Boy on a Goose*. Notice how she works with figure and display simultaneously to achieve a well-integrated final presentation.
Photos by Gerard Tolido

Solid Fimo fun sculptures by Maureen Carlson
Photo by Maureen Carlson

Where would *The Princess* be without the pea, the bed, and all the mattresses? Katherine Walmesley had to create the whole environment for her Cernit figure to tell the familiar story. Photo by Paul Shult

A Song For Chester, Super Sculpey, by Jodi and Richard Creager. All accessories—table, chair, gramophone, records, and ear trumpet—were completely handcrafted by Richard Creager. Photo by Richard Creager.

The figures and the furniture of Annie Wahl's *Amish Ladies Quilting* is so well scaled that, when photographed against the background of a real house, they appear to be the women next door. Photo by Annie Wahl

Dancing Lobster of Paperclay by Scott R. Gray. Photo by Scott R. Gray

Humpty Dumpty in Paperclay by Patricia Bibb
Photo by Nancy Walters

East Wind on Cherry Tree Lane, Paperclay, by Nancy Walters. This figure, bent back by the wind, presented support and balance problems for the artist. For the right look of motion, she sculpted the legs over rods which extend through the shoes and into the wooden base.
Photo by Nancy Walters

MATERIALS

UNDERSTANDING THE NEW CLAYS

The three parts of making a doll that I enjoy totally are the sculpture, the solution of the costume, and the final assembly. All the rest is necessary, but not as interesting. However, a dollmaker should understand the general principles of his chosen medium. As artists, we are more concerned with the final effect: what we need to know most is what the doll will look like, how to achieve that look, and what we should watch out for. Most of that you can learn here; the rest you will learn as you make decisions and experiment.

You can successfully use the polymer and paperclays without becoming a chemical engineer. For years, I wrapped Sculpey in paper towels to take up the oily residue that seemed to ooze from overly soft Sculpey. I didn't need to know that the oily stuff was the plasticizer, and I didn't need to know its chemical name. I just needed to know how to fix the problem so I could get on with the dollmaking business. I once talked at great length with a dollmaker who detailed any number of experiments she had made with mixing polymer clays, mixing paints into them, varying cooking times. After a bit, I began to wonder when she had time to actually make dolls, and I asked her how many she had made. She replied, somewhat surprised, that she had made only a few simple dolls for the purposes of her experimentations. She felt that she needed to know all about everything before she could make a real doll. All learning is commendable, but not when it gets in the way of making a doll! If you want to know how the materials work, use them and study as you go. The best experimentation happens on the way to a specific goal.

In order to start building your clay experience repertoire, you should play with your clays. When I first started to work with clay almost twenty years ago, I opened the box, rolled up a ball, grabbed the handiest tool—which happened to be a metal fingernail file—and started to make what I thought looked like a head. I did not stop to think about the material until I had made several dolls with it. Even then, I didn't think about it in depth until I had used another clay for comparison. Whether you have made dolls or used clays before, taking time to recognize some of the features will help you understand how to work the material better.

For the working dollmaker, this chapter presents a general understanding of the products and their reactions in simple terms. For an in-depth study of the polymer and paperclay products, their chemical natures and reactions, I recommend the discussions presented by Nan Roche in her book *The New Clay: Techniques and Approaches to Jewelry Making* and Mimi and Jim Winer in their book *Mimi's New Clays for Dollmaking*.

Rules as such in sculpture and dollmaking are really descriptions of what will happen with particular materials under certain sets of conditions. Polymer molecules will not fuse until the temperature of 275° F is maintained for fifteen minutes, and wet paperclay used with ungalvanized wire armatures will show rust stains: these descriptions are experiences shared by the manufacturers and users and presented as instructional material.

When we discuss any material, remember that, except for the original formulation of Fimo, none of these products was invented specifically for dollmaking. The polymer clays are by-products of industrial engineering, originally used for building scale models and design prototypes. They came to the home dollmaker through contacts with doll manufacturers and by being noticed in craft supply shops. Paperclay products were developed for the crafts market. The manufacturer does not care if you make decorative doorknobs or dolls. He can only say that his product will work for general applications under the conditions he prints in the instructions. He is not responsible for the temperature of *your* oven or home, nor is he able to consider what you mix or cover the product with. He is not responsible for the success or failure of *your* method of making fingers, or assembling armatures, or treating the surface. Most serious doll artists have gained more detailed knowledge about product application for dolls than the manufacturer.

THE OLD CLAYS

Before speaking about the new clays, let's look at the properties and types of old clays. They are, traditionally, the non-hardening, oil-based plasticines used for primary sculpture, and the water-based, kiln-fired ceramic clays. Wax and papier mâché can be loosely lumped in with this group, because they are also traditional modeling materials. All of these materials are very important in dollmaking.

Oil-based clays are used for direct sculptures that become the forms for molds. These clays cannot be hardened, but they are used for fine sculpture because they can be smoothed, detailed, and buried in wet plaster to make molds. The most familiar variety of plasticine clay is the type we all used in grade school. Plasticines used by artists are available in several varieties.

The water-based ceramic clays are simply a mixture of ground earths and clays. The low-fire coarser clays include terra cotta and pottery clay. The finer clays are used for porcelain; they require longer kiln firing at much higher temperatures. In dollmaking, low-fire clays were and are used to make china dolls, which are usually given a shiny glaze. The high-fire clays are used for matte porcelain (also called bisque) dolls. Water-based, kiln-fired clays can be used for direct sculpture: one-of-a-kind, not molded, direct from the hand of the artist. They can be made more liquid, to be poured into a mold, dried, and then fired. Molds, of course, allow the production of multiple identical pieces.

Wax, although not a clay, is also used to make direct sculpture and models for molds. Many artists who make molds for porcelain work do a first sculpture in plasticine clay, make a mold, then pour a wax casting from the mold. The wax casting is cleaned and tooled to take out any imperfections, then a final mold for casting porcelain is made from the wax model.

Shredded paper and ground paper pulp combined with water and sometimes glue (papier mâché) have also been used traditionally as modeling materials. Fine papier mâché, very wet, can be directly sculpted like clay. Papier mâché can also be pressed or pounded into plaster molds to make multiples.

THE NEW CLAYS

The modeling materials we discuss here—Sculpey, Fimo, Cernit, and the paperclays—are the new clays that closely resemble the traditional organic products but have been modernized by the addition of polymers, plasticizers and, in the case of Creative Paperclay, preservatives.

Polymer Clays

Sculpey® is a non-toxic, plastic-derived (resin-based) material that can be cured to a hard permanent finish in the low temperature of a home oven. For the specialist sculptor or dollmaker, it has most of the attributes of plasticine modeling clay. You can also have a hard original for molds if you wish; otherwise, just sculpt, cure, and finish one-of-a-kind originals. Sculpey, sometimes referred to as "regular," is usually white with a slightly granular feel.

Polyform® is another term for the material sold as Sculpey. Polyform is made by the same company and is usually seen in a more generic-looking box. Polyform is also available in eight-pound bulk boxes.

Open the box of Sculpey or Polyform and take out a marble-sized piece. Did it break, crumble, or crack? If it pulled like taffy or bubble gum before it separated, then it is in good working condition. Usable Sculpey will have some stretch before it tears. If it cracked, it might be slightly dry and, although somewhat stiff, it is usable. If it broke or crumbled, it is too dry to use. Dry Sculpey can be softened by heating slightly to about 100°. It can also be reconstituted with Sculpey Liquid Diluent®. I have found that, if the material can be worked in your hands until it is soft, you can proceed. If it requires more than that to reconstitute it, it's not worth using. When I encounter stiff Sculpey products that are still workable, I keep them for large, less detailed parts, such as the back of a head.

If you pull the white or colored Sculpey, it will stretch like taffy and tear rather than break. If you press the material between your fingers, it moves smoothly and quickly. You will also notice that it readily takes the impression of your fingerprints and has a dry, somewhat chalky feel. If you grasp it in your hand and squeeze it, it will ooze and take the impression of the folds of your palm rather sharply.

If you examine a stretched part and the tear, you will notice that, as the material stretches, it appears almost granular. If you rub it with your fingertips, it will readily smooth and take a slight shine. If you moisten your fingers and rub a rough edge, it will smooth down easily. If you press two pieces together and rub, it quickly blends so that no break shows. If you drag a tool to cut a curved line in the surface, the edges of the cut will be smooth and sharp. You will also notice that its dull surface allows it to pick up dirt quickly, almost marblizing the material as it is worked. From these observations, you can conclude that this material will not take much pressure in sculpting, with either fingers or tools, to make a sharp impression. You also observe that it can clean up with light rubbing or polishing, and that larger irregularities can be worked down with water. A mixture of equal parts Liquid Diluent and rubbing alcohol, applied with a soft brush, is a good finishing medium.

Super Sculpey® is also made by Polyform Products. It has the advantage of being much harder when cured. It comes in several flesh tones and, compared with regular Sculpey, it has a waxier surface appearance. It works up pretty much the same, although it is slightly stiffer under a tool. Cured Super Sculpey is far more difficult to carve, clean, and polish. Many doll artists, however, prefer it because there is less worry about breakage. On the other hand, for heads and hands, I have found that the modeling must be nearly perfect and finished before curing. It is just too hard to monkey around with Super Sculpey after it has been cured.

Super Sculpey seems to be fine for broad sculpture, but not so adaptable to fine detailing. It has a hard, cement-like finish when cured. In addition, it is also very difficult to paint, even with the most careful surface preparation. Many dollmakers prefer to let the cured clay stay as their basic flesh tone, detailing only the features with color. Artist Annie Wahl reports that blemishes ("flecking") which might occur on the surface result from moisture forming around resin particles; the manufacturer recommends Solid Softener/Dilutant be mixed in with the uncured material.

If you pull Super Sculpey, you will find that it takes more effort to pull than its sister products.

When it is stretched to the tearing point, it does not show any granulation. It will not show a fingerprint or a skin impression unless squeezed with considerable pressure. It looks and feels oily. If you work it between your fingers a minute, it will begin to feel sticky. If you rub it with your fingertips, it will quickly take on a surface shine. Water rubbed on the surface will smooth down larger bumps, but it will take more effort to make a smooth finish when two pieces are joined. If you drag a tool in a curve across the surface, the edges of the cut will show some roughness. From this you can observe that the material is going to require a little hand and tool pressure to make an impression. It is also going to resist small, soft detail work. It will take time to make a good blend when joining pieces.

When you have realized how the material works by observations like the above, you will not be as frustrated in working with it; you can adjust your approaches and choices accordingly. For instance, if I want to do a piece that has a lot of small, finely etched detail, I will use Sculpey and a somewhat dull tool like my metal fingernail file, to avoid cutting deeply or nicking the surface. If I want to do a piece that has relatively large, bland features, I will use Super Sculpey and a much finer tool, and I will be prepared to spend much more time in making a smooth finished surface. Those would be my choices, but they might not be yours.

Sculpey III® is the only Polyform product that comes in colors and, while it is versatile for the general hobbyist, it is not regularly used by dollmakers, who prefer to work out their own colors with more delicacy. Some artists will use brown Sculpey III for making dark flesh tones, but I have found that by itself it is too dark to read well. A maker would be well advised to experiment with mixing colors of Sculpey III to achieve satisfactory dark skin tones; the emphasis is on *experiment*. Expect to try a few times before you get to a solution that suits your design purpose.

Fimo® gained favor in the United States with dollmakers working with miniatures. Lately, it has been used increasingly by professional dollmakers, and successfully. It can be worked like modeling clay and can be cured in the home oven. Fimo comes in small colored blocks. Dollmakers mix colors and types to achieve differing flesh tones. Usually, the artist will paint or color only the detail features, leaving the natural cured surfaces as the base flesh. You should be aware of possible problems in mixing colors which might have different curing temperatures and times. It has been suggested that mixing types can cause mysterious white flecks to appear in the cured surface. It has also been suggested that the flecks result from air bubbles created during the blending. I do not have a solution for this, except to tell you to be aware of it. No product is perfect! You need to experiment to see which suits your needs best.

Cernit™ is a material favored recently by doll artists and miniaturists. It can be cured in boiling water as well as in an oven. Boiled Cernit has a rough, dull surface, whereas baked Cernit is more glazed. Like Fimo, Cernit is extremely resilient. Dollmakers sometimes use the term "melt" in conjunction with Cernit. It seems to melt when hand worked, and it seems to have a tendency to melt (expand, bubble) in the curing process.

Fimo and Cernit, as packaged, are hard blocks. It would almost require a hammer or a very strong downward pressure to make an impression on the surface. If you try to pull a piece off the block, you will find that it does not stretch; it immediately breaks and crumbles. For these products, this is normal behavior. As you try to work the material, you notice that it takes quite a bit of rubbing to join the crumbled bits into a smooth, malleable piece—about five minutes per square inch. In their working state, both are far more stretchy than Sculpey or Super Sculpey. They can be pulled several inches and very thinly before they will break. When you rub the material, it readily becomes glossy. Rubbing with moistened fingers will smooth rough areas. If two pieces are blended, it will take considerable effort to make the join smooth. Often such a join will involve only the surface layer of the material. Where the two pieces meet below the surface, they will probably not blend unless you work from the bottom of the hole outward. These uneven blends can trap air and cause surface checking in cooked pieces and, on occasion, cracking during curing. Avoid surface markings by being very careful to make completely joined additions in sculpting. It seems that some cracking and blistering in

any of the products is caused by foil armatures reflecting extra heat on the surrounding clay, or by air expanding inside the foil. Deep air pockets can be released by running a needle into the sculpted piece just prior to curing. Run the needle into the foil. Make several pricks in places that will not show on the finished piece.

In working with Fimo and Cernit, your approach will be much different than it would be for the Polyform products. I tend to think of Sculpey and Super Sculpey as "sculptable" materials, as material can be added much more easily. I think of Fimo and Cernit as more "modelable," as they are more successfully pushed or pressed into shape. In working with Fimo and Cernit, therefore, you would probably want to consider working more with your fingers and with dull tools such as wooden dowels, orange sticks, and toothpicks, unless you specifically want to cut the surface. In working these products, you would also want to take precautions against their resilience by working a thin amount over a rough armature, such as a loosely crumbled ball of foil: the foil surface will help grab the material.

Both Fimo and Cernit must be softened with the hands or the addition of softening agents. Some artists feel this is a nuisance, but two small packages can be brought to the working state by hand in about fifteen minutes. To do this, use clean hands and a clean working surface. With a sharp knife or tool, chop the block into tiny bits. Press and knead the bits and roll them together. Repeat chopping and rolling twice more. By the third kneading, the material should be softened so that it can be rolled into a sausage. Roll the sausage, fold it over, and re-roll until material is uniformly soft. If you are blending two colors, repeat the process until the color is uniform throughout.

Finally, note that lacquer-based paints directly applied to the surface of polymer clays do not dry.

Paperclays

Creative Paperclay® is a totally different type of material. It is basically water, paper pulp, talc, starch, and volcanic ash, with preservatives to keep moisture from causing mildew. It dries in open air and it is extremely strong, even in small, thin areas. As opposed to the polymer clays, paperclay works more like a water-based ceramic clay or plasticine.

It is not resilient, and pieces are easy to blend. It has no problem sticking to itself, wet to wet or wet to dry, and added material tends to stay where you put it. The best blend is achieved in joining wet to wet. With wet to dry, the dry part should be roughened. Composed of pulp fibers, when sculpted the fibers overlap, creating an almost woven structure. As opposed to ceramic clays, the wet material does not tend to slide. When dried, it can be sanded very smoothly or re-sculpted by carving or addition. It also takes any paint. As one artist said, "It is very difficult to fault this product."

No material is totally perfect, however. Paperclay is a *wet* product. That means that, unless sealed, it can become soggy when exposed to damp conditions. The wetness of the material also means that extra precautions must be taken. Paperclay does not work well over a bare wire armature. Use galvanized wire to avoid rust, and wrap wires with crumpled foil to provide grip. Next, make bones of paperclay and let them dry. When the skeleton is dry, add the final sculptural layers.

Other products: There are a number of similar products more or less available, such as Celluclay®, Friendly Clay™, Premier™, Crafty™, and La Doll™. You may wish to explore them on your own. I find them to be less workable than Creative Paperclay, so I leave them to your own adventurous spirits. Celluclay, for example, is considered to be stronger but dries rougher, and La Doll is more finely granulated.

TOXICITY

All of the polymers and paperclays can claim to be non-toxic. However, if you tend to be allergic to any part of the product, you could have a reaction. Dusty products like Celluclay and Creative Paperclay can get into your lungs. Wear a mask when working up dry paper products or when sanding. Otherwise, if you handle the materials as directed on the packages, you will probably not come to any physical grief. However, if the baby accidentally eats some craft clay or you dump it in the cookie dough, someone is likely to have a tummy problem. My Fimo package says it "may be harmful if swallowed." You should take care that none

of these products are eaten and, if so, call your physician or poison control hotline immediately. You should also take care to keep your clay cooking and curing utensils separate from your food preparation areas. It takes no big effort to designate one baking dish for your clay work. Do it!

With any product designated "non-toxic," it is expected that you know that means the product is not toxic if you use it as designed and as the manufacturers tell you to use it. If you do something else, it could become toxic. In the case of the polymer clays, most manufacturers tell you to make sure your cooking area is well ventilated. So, remember to turn on the fan or open a window when you have products in the oven. They tell you that the product can cause toxic vapors when heated above 350°. If they tell you that, it is probably true. Listen. Be in the kitchen while you cook, and keep an eye on the oven. What can it hurt? It does not take more than thirty minutes of your time, and usually less, to cook a batch of clay sculpture. What a terrific time to get your dishes washed or grab a quick sandwich. (But wash your hands first.)

When I first used Sculpey, I used Styrofoam as a head armature, and I wrote about doing so. I received a letter from a reader who told me that her husband, a fireman, warned that some such foams were toxic when heated or melted. I double-checked with my local fire marshal and, sure enough, he told me that the vapors given off were so toxic they would kill in one breath. This was enough to shift me to using foil as an armature rather quickly, I can tell you. And I did tell everyone else, too, in my classes and in my previous book on Sculpey. The warnings about Styrofoam have been passed through the dollmaking world. Now that you have read this, it will be your job to make sure you *don't use it*, and that you help us pass on the warning.

SHELF LIFE

When purchased, polymer Polyform products should be the consistency of oil-based modeling clays: soft and pliable. They should bend. If they break, their composition has probably deteriorated. We use the term "dried," but what we really mean is that the plasticizers have probably leached out, or that the material has been exposed to a temperature high enough to begin the curing process. Dry Sculpey is not the fault of the manufacturer. It is more likely caused by temperatures and time in shipping and storage from factory to distributor to retailer to you.

Occasionally, Sculpey will seem excessively soft. Some of us have thought that perhaps the manufacturer made the product a little softer for shipping during warm seasons. Soft Sculpey might be a little more difficult, but it is usable. If it is excessively soft, try refrigerating it for twenty minutes as you work. Crumbly Sculpey is not really usable. If yours seems to be coming that way, try to buy it from a dealer who turns over his stock regularly, or order it directly from the manufacturer. At home, take some precautions. Store your oven-curing clays in a cool place and double wrap them. Many artists routinely keep their modeling materials in the refrigerator.

I have mentioned that letting the product sit a month or more after purchase allows it to set up a bit more. We have also noticed that, if you wrap the product in paper towels, it will set up a bit faster. You might want to consider buying at regular intervals and using the oldest first. You also should be sure to check your stored Sculpey from time to time to see what is happening. All homes vary environmentally, and it seems all batches of clay vary somewhat. Be aware and pay attention to your product.

As noted, Fimo and Cernit are naturally a bit stiffer and more crumbly as they come out of the package. They seem to stay that way for a very long time. I am still using some that has been on my shelf, in opened packages, for almost seven years. Paperclay seems to maintain its moisture indefinitely in the sealed package. As soon as the package is opened, however, the product will begin to dry. Keep your opened paperclay well sealed in plastic bags or containers. Totally dry paperclay can be re-constituted by adding water, soaking a day or two, and mashing the clay back to a sloppy pulp.

For ease in working or re-constituting, the manufacturer of Fimo makes Mix Quick® that can be mixed in to make it more pliable, similar to Liquid Diluent. Polymer clays can be surface-smoothed with solvents such as acetone or fingernail polish remover. Neither should be used in large amounts, and both should be used only for small surfaces and in well-ventilated areas.

One last note regarding shelf-life: I still have a piece of uncooked Sculpey of good size from the first box I bought in 1975. (Yes, people were making dolls back then!) That piece has been stored in several different places, both warm and cool, and it is *still* workable, although incredibly dirty!

DURABILITY

In general, it is well to be concerned with making sure the products we use in dollmaking are sound. This is especially true if you are making delicate, complex figures that sell for hundreds of dollars. Dollmakers and collectors, however, need to remind themselves that *all* doll mediums are fragile. Porcelain can break and mildew, wood can dry, crack, and mildew, and cloth can rot, discolor, and decompose. It should be obvious that paper can turn to pulp when wet, apples can rot, and wax can melt. Rubber disintegrates. Compositions decompose and lose their painted finish. *There is no such thing as the perfect, permanent doll medium.*

The durability of a doll will depend on how it is treated during its existence. We have lovely museum collections in which dolls made of every material have survived two and three centuries of play and display. With all dolls, in almost every case of damage or deterioration, the cause is storage where the piece is subject to extreme temperature or humidity variations. A doll is more likely to be chewed by the family dog or soiled by dirty hands or falling dust than it is likely to fall apart because the material was not permanent.

I completed my first doll from Sculpey in 1975. Because it was my first, and because I wanted a very smooth glaze, and because no one warned me, I applied several layers of lacquer-based doll paint. When I got to the sixth coat, it began to dawn on me that lacquer-based paints were not going to dry on this material. I then painted on a few layers of gesso and used the lacquer over that. To this day I do not know what happened with the first few layers of paint: for all I know, they may still be sticky, but that doll is *exactly* like when I finished painting it. There has been no change in the surface. For several years, I have carried it around to classes as an example. It has had hard wear, but it has never broken. As a piece of art it is very amateur, but as a piece of polymer sculpture it has endured perfectly. Dutch artist Marleen Engeler told me that she had made a play doll of Cernit in 1979. After many years as a child's companion, it had to have its cloth body replaced, but no clay part has ever broken.

Between summer 1976 and spring 1977, I made ten more dolls of Sculpey. I have two of those dolls in my collection, and two more are in local collections. All of these dolls exhibit no change in material. It should be noted, however, that I routinely painted all exposed surfaces. Most of us did in those days. It is difficult to say if the coating of paint preserved the material. Since then, I have made over two hundred sculpted dolls with polymer clays, some painted, some not, several painted partly or with various paints.

Although the jungle drums of the doll world occasionally have tapped out messages that polymer clays shatter, I did not have a recorded case until recently. A dollmaker told me that one of her clients had a doll fall apart. As we talked, it came out that the owner had kept the doll in a sunny window. That explained the problem. Polymer products are sensitive to ultraviolet rays. Prolonged exposure to sunshine can cause the material to decompose. Most artists and collectors keep their dolls well out of the sun at all times, if only to protect the clothing from fading. If you do that and routinely warn those who have your work to keep the pieces out of the sunlight, there should be no problem with that type of deterioration.

All in all, oven-cured clays are relatively new products, and we really do not know what they will do over a hundred-year period. We do know that plastics and resins are not biodegradable, so it looks as if oven-cured clay dolls will be around for some time.

Paper-based products have been used by artists for at least two centuries. In the Orient, a substantial part of dollmaking is done with paper. So far as I can ascertain, none of these older dolls suffer any more or any less than wood or porcelain dolls over the long haul. The new paper-based products have not been on the market long enough to provide specific cases, but we have no reason to think that, if they are used thoughtfully and sealed well, they will not hold up as well.

As one artist said, the nature of dollmaking is dealing with problems. Each dollmaker will create a set of problems to be solved with each doll he wants to make and each medium he decides to use. The challenge of dollmaking is solving the problems and, in so doing, making a little person come to life.

Stella by Paul Robins
16", Paperclay over armature
Photo by Paul Robins

Boy on Fish by Lilian Tolido-Elzer
12", Paperclay
Photo by Gerard Tolido

Bird of Paradise by Paul Robins
14", Paperclay
Photo by Paul Robins

Off Duty Santa by Beth Cameron
18", Cernit and cloth over wire
Photo by John Wee

Welcome Aboard by Virginia Taylor
8", Super Sculpey
Photo by Virginia Taylor

Tailor, Little Elf with Teddy and *The Nutcracker* by Randi Taylor
3", Fimo and Cernit on cloth and wire armature
Photo by Nutshell News

The Gleaner by Kathy Gunson
33", Super Sculpey, cloth over wood
Photo by W. Donald Smith

Tix, Mr. Pim, Ned Cheerybal,
Max, Ernie, Isadore, and
There Was A Crooked Man
by Bill Nelson
13" to 17", Super Sculpey
and cloth over wire armature
Photo by Tim Gabbert

Boogie Woogie Bugle Boy of Company B by Jane Covington
17", Super Sculpey, cloth over wire armature
Photo by Bruce Bailey

Americana Election Year by Susanna Oroyan
20", Super Sculpey and cloth over wire armature
Photo by W. Donald Smith

Arlecchino by Patricia Brooks
14", Super Sculpey on wire armature
Photo by W. Donald Smith

Horse Singing His Song
by June Lunsford Goodnow
13", Super Sculpey and cloth
over wire armature
Photo by Brian Schul

Ix Chebel-Yax Mayan Goddess of Weaving (back)
by Betts Vidal
14", Fimo and cloth over wire armature
Photos by Betts Vidal

Ix Chebel-Yax Mayan Goddess of Weaving (front)

Pamina by Carol Nordell
15", Super Sculpey and cloth over wire armature
Photo by Tony Gezirjian

Untitled #1 by Bob and Anne Ross Anderson
20", Cernit and cloth over wire armature
Photo by Anne Ross Anderson

Untitled by Sandra Babin
16", Paperclay
Photo by Thomas L. Brown

Untitled by Sandra Babin
16", Paperclay
Photo by Thomas L. Brown

Dew Drop Faerie by Gail Lackey
9", Fimo and Sculpey
Photo by Gail Lackey

Cucumber Kid by Patricia Dugré Bibb
10", Super Sculpey, cloth, and Paperclay
Photo by Nancy Walters

Grandmother Gall by Susanna Oroyan
15", Paperclay
Photo by W. Donald Smith

Flossie-Flora and *Off Duty Santa* by Katherine Paiva
18", Sculpey and cloth
Photo by W. Donald Smith

Anika by Kim Brown
27", Super Sculpey and cloth over wire armature
Photo by Kim Brown

Vera Vane and *Buffy Knickerbocker Van Beek*
by Susanna Oroyan
18", Sculpey
Photo by W. Donald Smith

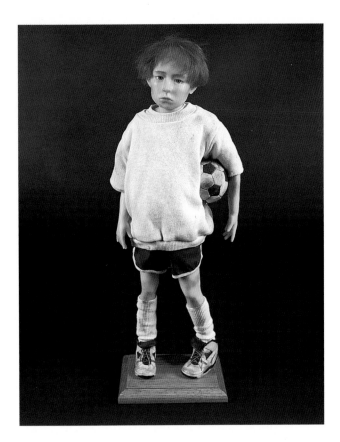

Sad Boy with Soccer Ball by Carol Trobe
19½", Cernit
Photo by Terrence McGarrigle

Forever Friends by Linda Kertzman
12", Super Sculpey, Cernit, cloth over wire
Photo by Linda Kertzman

Little Girl in Red Sandals by Carol Trobe
18", Cernit and cloth over wire armature
Photo by Terrence McGarrigle

Teapot Lady by Scott R. Gray
27", Paperclay and teapot
Photo by Scott R. Gray

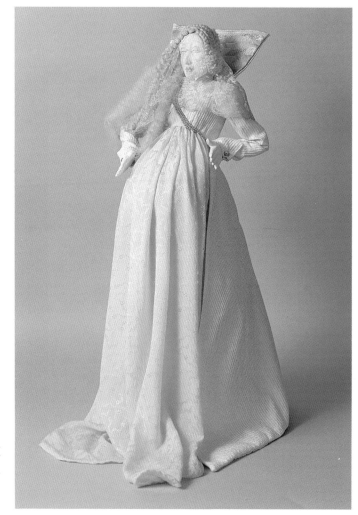

Empress Expectant by Susanna Oroyan
25", Paperclay
Photo by W. Donald Smith

All That Jazz by Van Craig
22", papier mâché over wire armature
Photo by Malcolm J. Magri

Class Reunion—Sweet Revenge by Toni Carroll
21", Cernit head and hands, Paperclay legs,
cloth over wire armature
Photo by J. G. Nash

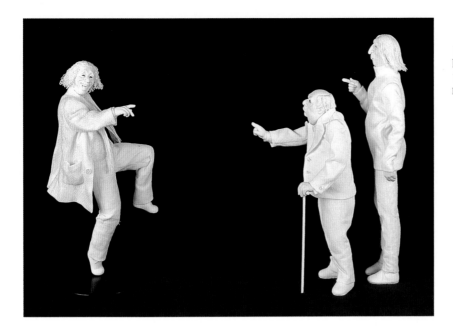

Without Words
by Elisabeth Flueler-Tomamichel
10", Super Sculpey
Photo by W. Donald Smith

Chelsey Babe by Marilyn Stauber
10", Cernit
Photo by Marilyn Stauber

Lissa and Her Dragon by Lisa Lichtenfels
42", Super Sculpey
Photo by Lisa Lichtenfels

APPENDICES

DOLL CLUBS

Purpose: To show, share, learn, and enjoy being with others who love to make dolls.

Finding members: Often a colorful poster with a sign-up sheet, displayed in your local craft or fabric shop, will draw interested people. You might also place an invitation on your local newspaper's events page. Plan an exhibit of hand-made dolls at a shop or mall, and have a sign-up sheet available. Do not limit your group to people with only one dollmaking interest. Everyone will learn more in a diverse group: cloth, porcelain, and creative clay dollmaking.

Size of group: The number of members will be determined by the nature of your meetings. If the group prefers hands-on project work, the meeting place will need adequate worktable space. Meetings in members' homes are fun because you are able to see each other's collections and work in progress; however, in most cases, it is not easy or feasible actually to work on projects there. The ideal situation is one where you have a public facility—a shop or community room—on a regular basis; reserve members' homes for special occasions.

Time: When you get a core group together, you will need to heed preferences for day or evening meetings. If the needs are split because of home or work obligations, you might form two groups, even if each one is small. It is better for a group to grow than to have people drop out because they cannot make the meetings.

Organizing: You will need a co-ordinator to conduct meetings and organize activities, a program chairman, a secretary for telephoning or sending postcards, and a treasurer to keep simple accounting of any dues or project income and expenses.

Meetings: Don't be afraid of structure. A typical meeting might begin with discussion of business, news, and general planning. A new group might want to follow this with "life histories": at each meeting, one or two members briefly tell about their background, experiences, and dollmaking interests. All club meetings should include "show and tell." All members show what they have made, or tell something they have learned, or share any special information that might not be directly related to the business or program portion of the meeting.

Club Projects: As your group develops, new interests, materials, and ideas will arise for programs or projects. It is a good idea for the secretary to provide each member with the program schedule and a membership phone list. Essentially, all club projects are learning experiences. One person should be responsible for presenting background information or technical information for the meeting's topic. Others bring in dolls they have made to follow the theme. Here are some suggestions:

January: Things with wings! Create an elf, fairy, or even a prince riding a dragon.

February: Sugar and spice and everything nice, this is the month to talk about ribbons and lace and trims. A project could involve the creative use of fancy materials, or making trims and accessories.

March: How about hair? See how many materials can be used for doll hair and wigs—from traditional mohair to sponges, buttons, and wire. See who can be the most outrageously creative, and award prizes.

April: Spring brings baby things. Take a look at baby dolls, the many ways to make and show them. Fine hand-sewing techniques and embroidery stitches might be demonstrated.

May: Flowers, of course. Make a doll with May baskets, or a group of small dolls dancing around a May pole. Investigate creative applications of dried and silk flowers.

June: Brides or dolls in white costumes. Remember, not all brides are pretty and young. Develop an unusual character.

July and *August:* If you take a summer break, a long-term project might be making a peddler doll and finding miniature merchandise: a fruit peddler, a notion nanny, a basket peddler, a pot-and-pan man, a flower vender....

September: Start a Round Robin doll project. This is loosely based on the "friendship quilt" idea. Each person makes one basic doll (cloth or sculpted parts) with painted face. Dolls are placed in a brown bag and passed: each gets another's doll. They return with the doll wigged the next month. The dolls are bagged and passed each month, until shoes, underwear, costume, accessories, and background or base are completed. At the end of the project, your doll comes back to you as a surprise!

October: Halloween suggests a challenge to bring a doll holding or wearing a mask, whether Halloween, Mardi Gras, animal, or fancy dress.

November: Start preparing the season with a doll Christmas ornament or decoration. Perhaps the challenge can be an inventive Santa.

December: Since everyone is busy, make a mini-doll or a doll pin, and have an exchange of them.

Continuing Projects

The Annual Exhibit: If your group is meeting in or working through a shop, you should definitely display the projects you have made during the year. Work with the owner or manager to create a pleasing display of instructional materials and available classes.

Exhibits can be held anywhere you can show your dolls attractively and securely. Think about shopping malls, office-building lobbies, senior centers, and banks. Perhaps you can work with a church group to present an exhibit in conjunction with a Mother's Day Tea or Annual Bazaar. If all else fails, do what elinor peace bailey does once a year: put all the dolls you can get in a member's home, open the doors, and invite the world!

Public Service: Take dolls to hospital children's wards or rest homes for show and tell. Provide dollmaking activities for youth groups, take your dolls to school, and don't forget the Girl Scouts award a doll-collecting badge.

Competitions: Eventually the idea of having a competitive exhibit with judges and ribbons will come up. This is a fine activity if you remember that there are two very different types of competition. One is the "judge's choice" and the other a "critical ranking." Misunderstanding or mixing the two can be deadly. Make a firm decision on which type your competition is to be, and make sure all entrants are aware of the nature of the judging.

Judge's choice: The judges look at a group or category and decide which dolls they like best, in a ranked order. There are awards for best, second, third, and possibly honorable mention. Here, the decision should be based on a real understanding of the work on a design or technical basis, but too often it is not: judges are visiting dignitaries from other fields who do not themselves make dolls or who are unfamiliar with doll art standards. Sometimes, this event is a "people's choice": the decisions are based on what appeals to the judge or voters. The entrant should be aware that the decisions do not often reflect anything but what a given person feels at a certain time. It is more a popularity contest than a learning experience. It is fun, but it is not to be taken seriously as an authorization of excellence.

The critical ranking: In this judging, the works are awarded points for up to ten criteria. Judges are carefully selected as not only fine doll artists themselves, but people familiar with art and design. In a critical jurying, it is possible for all the dolls in a category to get a first-place ribbon if they all demonstrate first-class work and score enough points. It is, however, also possible for no doll to receive a first-place ranking. A judge in this situation will be looking for fine details of workmanship, such as paint finish, anatomical detail, proportion, scale in costume design, and originality. A score card with points possible for each criterion and points awarded is given to each entrant. Judges may hold a follow-up seminar to discuss their scoring, so that each entrant actually learns where his work might be improved. This experience can be educational for the serious dollmaker, if judges are selected who are both well versed in the dollmaking arts and respected in the field. Examples of scoring methods for this type of judging can be found in the books *Judging Dolls* by Mildred Seeley and *Dollmaker's Notebook: Competition and Critique* by Susanna Oroyan.

ORGANIZATIONS

Send a stamped addressed envelope with all inquiries.

Doll Artisans Guild
(Newsletter, annual meeting, competitive exhibits)
Seeley Ceramics Services, Inc.
9 River Street
Oneonta, NY 13820

United Federation of Doll Clubs
(Quarterly magazine, local clubs, national and regional conferences, emphasis on collecting)
10920 North Ambassador Drive
Kansas City, MO 64153

National Institute of American Doll Artists (NIADA)
(Juried artist membership, annual conference open to all)
Elsie Orr
2600 Leix Way
South San Francisco, CA 94080

Original Doll Artist Council of America (ODACA)
(Juried membership, annual seminar and show)
Brenda Stewart
1562 Rooker Road
Morrisville, IN 46158

International Dollmaker's Association (IDMA)
(Newsletter, annual conference)
Lucille Gerrard
16770 Wilderness Court
Jackson, CA 95642

British Doll Artist Association (BDA)
(Juried membership, annual exhibits. Please send two international postal reply coupons.)
Jane Davies
Amber, The Street
Walburton, Arundel
Sussex, England BN1 80PH

The Australian Doll Journal
(Please send two international postal reply coupons.)
Box 680
Goulburn
New South Wales
Australia 2580

MAGAZINES

Dollmaking is, by and large, a solitary occupation. Most people begin on their own but, when they find there are others in the world who do what they do, they are eager to learn more. I suggest you sample the periodicals and keep up with those that most nearly fit your dollmaking interests.

Contemporary Doll Magazine and
Doll Crafter Magazine
Scott Publications
30595 Eight Mile Road
Livonia, MI 48152

Dolls, the Collector's Magazine
Acquire Publications
170 Fifth Avenue, 12th Floor
New York, NY 10010

Dollmaker's Journal
2900 West Anderson Lane, #20-150
Austin, TX 78757

Doll Reader Magazine
Cumberland Publishing
900 Frederick Street
Cumberland, MD 21502

Doll Designs and *International Doll World*
House of White Birches
306 East Parr Road
Berne, IN 46711

Newsletter
Association for People Who Like to Play with Dolls
1779 East Avenue
Hayward, CA 94145

BOOKS

A dollmaker can never have or read enough books. From books we learn about what other dollmakers have done and are doing, as well as the technical processes associated with our craft. The list below, by no means complete, will give you quick access to the basic and best available information in all areas of dollmaking. It includes my own favorite references and several works recommended by the other artists in this book. When writing to a self-published author, do enclose a stamped addressed envelope for the return of ordering information.

As you explore the world of dollmaking you will also find a number of books on library shelves or in dealers' catalogues that feature the work of individual doll artists or related areas of dollmaking, such as cloth or carved wood. Look at everything and anything about dollmaking. Even if a work does not pertain to your specific interest, it may contain something applicable or adaptable. Remember that many technical processes used by dollmakers are drawn from "real-world" skills, from forging metals to feathering millinery. Inspiration and insight can also come from the study of works on design, sculpture, painting, theater, and fiber arts. Look and learn!

Alexander, Lyn. *Make Doll Shoes!* Cumberland, MD: Hobby House Press. Workbooks. 2 volumes
— *Pattern Designing for Dressmakers.* Cumberland, MD: Hobby House Press.

Armstrong-Hand, Martha. *Mold Making.* (Martha Armstrong-Hand, 575 Worcester Drive, Cambria, CA 93428)
— *Doll Articulation.*

Arnold, Janet. *Patterns of Fashion.* London: MacMillan, 1982. 3 volumes

Bailey, Elinor Peace. *Mother Plays With Dolls.* McLean, VA: EPM, 1990.

Bradfield, Nancy. *Costume in Detail: 1730-1930.* London: Harrap, 1982.

Brooks, Patricia Ryan. Babes in Wood: *An Introduction to Doll Carving.* (Patricia Ryan Brooks, 248 East Vineland Road, Augusta, GA 30904)

Bullard, Helen. *The American Doll Artist.* (Volume I) Boston: Charles T. Branford, 1965. (Volume II) Kansas City, MO: Athena, 1975.

Carlson, Maureen. Videotapes on working with polymer clays. (Wee Folk Creations, 18476 Natchez Avenue, Prior Lake, MN 55372)

Cely, Antonette. *Creating Your Own Fabric.* (PO Box 52043, Atlanta, GA 30355)

Engeler, Marleen. *Sculpting Dolls in Cernit.* Livonia, MI: Scott Publications, 1991.

Erickson, Rolf and Faith Wick. *Sculpting Little People.* Oneonta, NY: Seeley Ceramic Services, 1988. 2 volumes

Faigen, Gary. *The Artist's Complete Guide to Facial Expressions.* New York: Watson-Guptill, 1990.

Grubbs, Daisy. *Modeling a Likeness in Clay: Step-by-Step Techniques for Capturing Character.* New York: Watson-Guptill, 1982.

Gunzel, Hildegard. *Creating Original Porcelain Dolls.* Cumberland, MD: Hobby House Press, 1988.

Hamm, Jack. *Drawing the Head and Figure.* New York: Grosset & Dunlap, 1967.
— *Cartooning the Head and Figure.* New York: Grosset & Dunlap, 1963.

Kinzie, Sharon. *How to Paint Eyes.* Livonia, MI: Scott Publications, 1989.

Laury, Jean Ray. *Dollmaking: A Creative Approach.* New York: Van Nostrand Reinhold, 1970.

Luccesi, Bruno. *Modeling the Head in Clay.* New York: Watson-Guptill, 1979.

McFadden, Sybil. *Fawn Zeller's Porcelain Dollmaking Techniques.* Cumberland, MD: Hobby House Press, 1984.

McKinley, Robert. *Dollmaking: One Artist's Approach*. (Nelson/McKinley Books, 107 East Cary Street, Richmond, VA 23219)

Miller, Richard McDermott. *Figure Sculpture in Wax and Plaster*. New York: Watson-Guptill, 1971.

National Institute of American Doll Artists. *The Art of the Doll*. 1992. (Barrie, Route 1, Box 9640, Loomis Hill Road, Waterbury Center, VT 05677)

Nunn, Joan. *Fashion in Costume 1200-1980*. London: Herbert, 1984.

Oroyan, Susanna. *Dollmaker's Notebook: Competition and Critique*. 1993. (Fabricat Designs, 3270 Whitbeck Boulevard, Eugene, OR 97405)
— *Dollmaker's Notebook: Working With Contracts*. 1993.
— *Dollmaker's Notebook: Working With Paperclay*. 1992.
— *Dollmaker's Notebook: Working With Polymer Clays*. 1993.

Oroyan, Susanna and Carol-Lynn Rossel Waugh. *Contemporary Artist Dolls: A Guide For The Collector*. Cumberland, MD: Hobby House Press, 1986.

Richter, Joachim. *Kunstlerpuppen*. Munich: Magica Lanterna Press, 1986 and 1989. 2 volumes

Roche, Nan. *The New Clay: Techniques and Approaches to Jewelry Making*. Rockville, MD: The Flower Valley Press, 1991.

Schmahl, Marion. *Kunstobjekt Puppe*. Ravensburg, Germany: Weingarten, 1990.

Schrott, Rotraut. *Making Original and Portrait Dolls in Cernit*. Cumberland, MD: Hobby House Press, 1993.

Seeley, Mildred. *Judging Dolls*. Livonia, MI: Scott Publications, 1991.

Stuart, George. Videotape on making historical figures (Stuart, PO Box 508, Ojai, CA 93024)

Whelpley, Alice and Lee. *Doll Workshop*. Cumberland, MD: Hobby House Press. 8 volumes covering, wax, mold making, composition, and costuming, published over several years

Winer, "Mimi" and Jim. *Mimi's New Clays for Dollmaking*. Point Pleasant, NJ: 1993. (Books and Supplies, PO Box 662, Point Pleasant, NJ 08742)

Book Distributors

Write for catalogue of titles available.

Hobby House Press
900 Frederick Street
Cumberland, MD 21502

Scott Publications
30595 Eight Mile Road
Livonia, MI 48152

THE ARTISTS

I would like to thank my artist friends who most kindly took time to share the photos of their work, their dollmaking ideas, resources, and solutions with me during the writing of this book. If you would like to contact them regarding purchase of dolls, arrangement of classes, or potential exhibits, please write to them at these addresses. Enclose a stamped addressed envelope to insure a prompt response.

* indicates artists who offer tutoring or classes

Anderson, Bob and Anne Ross
4022 Blackhawk Road
Rock Island, IL 61204

Babin, Sandra
515 West Main Street
Houma, LA 70360

Baker, Betsey
RR 2, Box 87
Cold Spring, NY 10516

*Bibb, Patricia Dugré
247 Overlook Drive
Chuluota, FL 32766

*Brooks, Patricia
248 East Vineland Road
Augusta, GA 30904

*Brown, Kim
5304 Cottonwood Club Circle
Salt Lake City, UT 84117

Cameron, Beth
1000 Washington
Oakmont, PA 15139

*Carlson, Maureen
18476 Natchez Avenue
Prior Lake, MN 55372

Carroll, Toni
489 Blackwood Drive
Longwood, FL 32750

Conrad, Holly
84 East River Bend Road
Fredericksburg, VA 22407

*Covington, Jane
707 Cuttle Road
Marysville, MI 48040

Craig, Van
417 West 46th Street
New York, NY 10036

Creager, Jodi and Richard
105 Berryman Street
Grass Valley, CA 95945

Cronin, Nancy
90 Main Street
North Reading, MA 01864

*Dunham, Susan
36429 Row River Road
Cottage Grove, OR 97424

Elder, Linda Lunsford
2324 Ashley Drive
Oklahoma City, OK 73120

Engeler, Marleen
Noordeinde 67
1141AH Monnickendam, Netherlands

Finch, Margaret
106 Liberty Avenue
New Rochelle, NY 10805

Finch-Kozlosky, Marta
9 Catamount Lane
Old Bennington, VT 05201

Flueler-Tomamichel, Elisabeth
Bodenacherstrasse 87
CH8121 Benglen, Switzerland

Gill, Linda
645 Southwind Drive
El Centro, CA 92243

*Goodnow, June Lunsford
2324 Ashley Drive
Oklahoma City, OK 73120

*Gray, Scott R.
1101 17th Avenue, #308
Seattle, WA 98122

*Gunson, Kathy
91250 River Road
Junction City, OR 97448

*Katin, Hedy
572 Edelweiss Drive
San Jose, CA 95136

*Kertzman, Linda
37 West Main Street
Morris, NY 13808

Klawitter, Judith
2303 River Road
Missoula, MT 59801

*Kolesar, Pat
21 North Limestone Street
Jamestown, OH 45335

Lackey, Gail
11716 Emerald Road
Nampa, ID 83686

*Lady, Barbara
325 Quarry Road
Albany, OR 97321

*Lampi, Sally
2261 Beckham Way
Hayward, CA 94541

*Lichtenfels, Lisa
PO Box 90537
Springfield, MA 01139

Maris, Eunice
120 West Pennsylvania Avenue
DeLand, FL 32720

*McKinley, Robert
17 Jane Street, #17E
New York, NY 10014

Munger, Ray
10061 Robin Hood Court
King George, VA 22485

Nelson, Bill
107 East Carey Street
Richmond, VA 23219

*Nordell, Carol
368 East Fifth Street
Mount Vernon, NY 10553

*Oroyan, Susanna
3270 Whitbeck Boulevard
Eugene, OR 97405

Paiva, Katherine
10319 244th Street
Edmonds, WA 98020

Poitras, Ellen
PO Box 574123
Orlando, FL 32857

Radzat, Marilyn
PO Box 299
Valley Ford, CA 94972

*Robins, Paul
Box 28, Site 14, RR#1
Gabriola Island, BC
Canada V0R 1X0

Shaughnessy, Sharon "Dee"
315 Front Beach, R #4
Ocean Springs, MS 39564

Stauber, Marilyn
2263 University Street
Eugene, OR 97403

*Stuart, George
PO Box 508
Ojai, CA 93024

Taylor, E. J.
6 Layer Gardens
Acton W3 9PR
London, England

Taylor, Randi
10222 Kaimu Drive
Huntington Beach, CA 92646

Taylor, Virginia
(address withheld by request)

Tolido-Elzer, Lilian
Trianglestraat 18
2287 TS Rijswijk
Netherlands

Trobe, Carol
116 Mainsail Drive
Grayslake, IL 60030

*Vidal, Betts
26163 Underwood Avenue
Hayward, CA 94544

Volpi, Rosemary
13227 W. Exposition Drive
Lakewood, CO 80228

Wahl, Annie
10330 Upper 196 Street W
Lakeville, MN 55042

*Walmsley, Kathryn
8041 Shady Road
Oldenburg, IN 47036

*Walters, Nancy
690 Trinity Court
Longwood, FL 32750

Wingerd-Graham, Linda
3765 7th Court South
Salem, OR 97302

Artists' work may be seen at:

All Our Children, Pewaukee, WI

Antique and Modern Doll Shop, Decatur, IN

Artist's Doll, Palo Alto, CA

Artistic Hand, Oviedo, FL

Cedar Rose Lane, Big Bear, CA

Enchanted Room, North Hammondsport, NY

Gigi's Dolls and Sherri's Bears, Chicago, IL

Mann Gallery, Boston, MA

Museum of Doll Art, Bellevue, WA

Petite Elite Museum of Miniatures, Century City, CA

Riki Schaffer Gallery, West Bloomfield, MI

Strong Museum, Rochester, NY

Swiss Doll Museum, Stein am Rhein, Switzerland

Toy Shoppe, Midlothian, VA

Turner Doll Shop, Bloomington, IN

Ventura County Museum of History and Art,
    Ventura, CA

We Two, Fairbanks, AK

ADVICE FOR BEGINNERS

George Stuart: The best method is to start at age three with mashed potatoes and work on from there. The trick to all of this is to work on it for forty years.

Virginia Taylor: Just do it, pick a medium and play with it, even if to try something for a Christmas gift, but don't wait until Christmas.

Betsey Baker: Make dolls because you love the work and the feeling of accomplishment with having turned an idea into a work of art.

Jane Covington: Michelangelo didn't learn it all at once, either.

Ray Munger: Recharge often, share your life with other dollmakers, never give up.

Stories from the Combat Zone

Whenever dollmakers get together or talk to each other, there are shared stories of the mysterious, spooky, and miraculous. Many of these happenings center on Lisa Lichtenfels, who makes life-sized needlesculpted figures. Take the time she was in the process of loading a big figure into a client's car, when suddenly she was surrounded by a police SWAT team, guns drawn, shouting at her to "Drop the body, lady." Or the time she spent a very frustrating week working on the mouth of a portrait piece. It refused to work right, so she finally pinned it shut and went on to work on something else. After a few more days she returned to the piece and finished it with no trouble. Later, she learned that the human whose portrait she was doing had had minor surgery on her mouth the very same week.

In the realm of spooky, there are always the instant glue horror stories. We all tend to use our mouths as a third hand. One artist, needing to free up her hand, stuck the object with the super glue in her mouth and promptly glued her tongue to the top of her mouth. Terribly embarrassing to have to explain at the hospital emergency room at 2 AM. Lesson to be learned, kids: watch what you put in your mouths.

Most of us are aware of the "oven spirits" and what mysterious things can happen when sculptures are cured, like Virginia Taylor's unidentified plain brown clay coming out of the oven with brown polka dots: "Not at all what I expected, but it ended up being one of my favorite pieces." That clay, by the way, was probably Westwood Ovencraft Clay®, which does freckle as it cures.

We don't often have the Paul Robins's "mysterious on-growing sparkles," either. His photographer commented about sparkles on the surface of a figure, making it difficult to light. "I had not put any sparkles in the finish, but what had happened was that salts in a fabric dye used as an emergency finish had seeped out, forming tiny crystals anywhere the overglaze had been applied. As I write, the crystals are still growing!"

And then there is Randi Taylor's "sideways success" story. "I was making a tray of caramel-colored Fimo teddy bears at Christmas time, and my best friend came over. Before I could say anything, she popped a few of the freshly baked clay teddies in her mouth."

Never a dull moment in dollmaking!

PHOTO STUDY EXERCISES

Successful dollmaking is learned as much by studying other dolls as by actually making dolls. The following exercises are geared to help the beginning dollmaker learn to analyze and integrate design and construction approaches. Take pencil and paper and answer the questions.

Santas

On pages 11–12, I show several versions of both Santa and Father Christmas figures.

> What are the three different types of headgear?
> Which figure uses a unique hand treatment? What is it?
> Are all the beard treatments the same? How do they differ?

Find as many unusual finishing details or embellishments as you can.

Faces

For each face, write the emotion or idea it seems to convey (silly, serene, thoughful, etc.). Then, write a few words describing how each artist has sculpted that emotion or idea (eyes closed, big grin, furrowed brow, relaxed muscles). In some cases, the finish or painting underscores the idea. Note special treatments you think are effective in conveying the idea of character.

Photo Section

Cinderella's Stepmother (page 56)
> How is this portrayal different from the traditional? The stepmother is supposed to be mean and cruel. How is this shown?

Americana Election Year (page 101)
> What country is represented? How do you know? How else?
> What secondary or non-obvious elements indicate the country?
> Why would this figure have a green-tinted face?
> What statement is the figure making?
> Do you have a strong reaction?

The group of seven figures created by Bill Nelson (page 100)
> Who are these guys? Can you describe a set of personality traits for each one?

There are two Native American figures shown (pages 59 and 102). If you were a collector, why would you buy them?

Sara, Mother Earth, and Hagglinda (pages 53 and 54) all depict older or elderly faces. How does each artist create the illusion of age? Compare these figures to the face of Marjory by E.J. Taylor (page 49).

If too much hair is a problem on a doll, how is it that Marilyn Radzat (page 55) is able to use an abundance and still have a very effective look?

Only one figure is shown with full back detail (page 103). What do you think the backs of the other figures look like?

Carol Nordell's figure (page 104) is only 15" tall. What fabrics did she have to find in order to make the costume look correct?

Find figures which have combined two or more very unexpected elements or details. What are the effects of such combinations?

Elisabeth Flueler-Tomamichel created a grouping of three figures all done in white (page 111). What elements underscore the static figures? Design layout or position also makes a statement. Consider how she arranged these figures.

Almost every figure is shown in motion or doing something. Are there any not in motion? Are you sure?

Find two figures that show sheer joy. How do the artists convey that emotion?

Find three fantasy figures. Describe the elements used to tell the viewer that these are imaginative or "unrealistic."

Robert McKinley's Innkeeper's Wife (page 51)
What is the body posture supposed to tell you? What do the hair style and stockings have to do with the characterization? Find three ways in which the costume has been made to underscore the posture or motion. What would have been the effect if the artist had chosen to use brightly colored calico fabrics?

Class Reunion (page 110)
What do the accessories tell you? What is the revenge? If you didn't know the name of this figure, would you still know its story? If you took away the accessories, would the figure alone tell the story?

Virginia Taylor (page 99) and Katherine Paiva (page 107) have done very simple forms. Should they have added more detail? If not, why not?

Find a figure that does *not* impress you. Compare it with one that does. What are the differences? What should or could be done to improve the less impressive figure?

SUPPLIES

A dollmaker can use just about anything and everything in the making of a doll. The following list will provide initial contacts for creating a supply base. To become more knowl-edgeable and to keep current with the full range of media and materials, investigate catalogues available from suppliers who advertise in the dollmaker publications.

Clays

Cernit, La Doll, Premier, and *Crafty*
Handcraft Designs, Inc.
63 East Broad Street
Hatfield, PA 19440

Creative Paperclay
Creative Paperclay Products
1800 South Robertson Boulevard
Los Angeles, CA 90035

Fimo and *Cernit*
The Clay Factory
PO Box 1270
Escondido, CA 92025

La Doll
Kim Lincoln
410 Bell Avenue
Santa Ana, CA 92707

Sculpey and *Polyform*
Polyform Products
9420 Byron Street
PO Box 2119
Schiller Park, IL 60176

General Sculpture Materials

American Art Clay Co., Inc.
4717 W. 16th Street
Indianapolis, IN 46222

New York Central Art Supply
62 Third Avenue
New York, NY 10003

Sax Arts and Crafts
PO Box 2002
Milwaukee, WI 53021

General Dollmaking Supplies

Mimi's Books and Supplies for the Serious Dollmaker
PO Box 662
Point Pleasant, NJ 08742

Playhouse Import Export, Inc.
25377 Huntwood Avenue
Hayward, CA 94544

Celluclay and Celluclay II are registered trademarks of Activa Products, Inc.

Cernit is a trademark of T&F GmbH, Dreieich, Germany.

Claystone is a registered trademark of Sculpture House, Inc.

Crafty, La Doll, and Premier are products of Padico.

Creative Paperclay is a trademark of Creative Paperclay Company, Inc.

DAS Pronto Clay is distributed in the U.S. by Battat, Adica Pongo Division.

Fimo and Mix Quick are registered trademarks of Eberhardt-Faber, Neumarkt, Germany, and are distributed in the U.S. by American Art Clay Company.

Friendly Clay is a product of American Art Clay Company.

Helen's Powder is a product of Dr. R. + H. Muntwyler, Germany.

Jewelry Glaze is a product of Delta Technical Coatings, Inc.

Liquitex is a registered trademark of Binney & Smith, Inc.

Lycra and Mylar are registered trademarks of E. I. duPont de Nemours & Company.

Ovencraft Clay is a registered trademark of Laguna Clay Company.

Pigma Micron is a registered trademark of Sakura Color Products Corporation of America.

Poly-fil and Traditional Needlepunched Polyester Batting are registered trademarks of Fairfield Processing Corporation.

Polyform, Sculpey, Super Sculpey, Sculpey III, and Liquid Diluent are registered trademarks of Polyform Products.

Styrofoam Brand Insulation is a registered trademark of Dow Chemical.

Ultrasuede is a registered trademark of Springs Industries, Inc.

ABOUT THE AUTHOR

Susanna Oroyan began making dolls seriously in 1972. At that time, there were no classes available and few instructional books, so she taught herself and experimented widely. Although she began primarily with cloth dolls, in 1975 a friend introduced her to Sculpey, and she soon began combining polymer sculpture with cloth. Since then, she has made about 500 dolls, and her dollmaking has grown into a full-time career and a business.

For the past decade she has been a motivating force in regional and national dollmakers' organizations, she has exhibited her dolls internationally, and she has written several books and well over a hundred articles for doll magazines. She has also taught dollmaking classes at many major seminars as well as for individual dollmaking groups. Her cloth-doll patterns are sold by Fabricat Designs, 3270 Whitbeck Boulevard, Eugene, OR 97405.

OTHER FINE CRAFTS BOOKS
FROM C & T PUBLISHING

An Amish Adventure, Roberta Horton

Appliqué 12 Easy Ways! Elly Sienkiewicz

Appliqué 12 Borders and Medallions, Elly Sienkiewicz

The Art of Silk Ribbon Embroidery, Judith Montano

Baltimore Album Quilts, Historic Notes and Antique Patterns, Elly Sienkiewicz

Baltimore Album Revival! Historic Quilts in the Making. The Catalog of C&T Publishing's Quilt Show and Contest

Baltimore Beauties and Beyond (2 Volumes), Elly Sienkiewicz

The Best From Gooseberry Hill: Patterns For Stuffed Animals & Dolls, Kathy Pace

Calico and Beyond, Roberta Horton

A Celebration of Hearts, Jean Wells and Marina Anderson

Christmas Traditions From the Heart, Margaret Peters

Christmas Traditions From the Heart, Volume Two, Margaret Peters

A Colorful Book, Yvonne Porcella

Crazy Quilt Handbook, Judith Montano

Crazy Quilt Odyssey, Judith Montano

Design a Baltimore Album Quilt! Elly Sienkiewicz

Dimensional Appliqué—Baskets, Blooms & Borders, Elly Sienkiewicz

14,287 Pieces of Fabrics and Other Poems, Jean Ray Laury

Friendship's Offering, Susan McKelvey

Happy Trails, Pepper Cory

Heirloom Machine Quilting, Harriet Hargrave

Imagery on Fabric, Jean Ray Laury

Isometric Perspective, Katie Pasquini-Masopust

Landscapes & Illusions, Joen Wolfrom

The Magical Effects of Color, Joen Wolfrom

Mariner's Compass, Judy Mathieson

Mastering Machine Appliqué, Harriet Hargrave

Memorabilia Quilting, Jean Wells

The New Lone Star Handbook, Blanche Young and Helen Young Frost

NSA Series: Bloomin' Creations, Jean Wells

NSA Series: Holiday Magic, Jean Wells

NSA Series: Hometown, Jean Wells

NSA Series: Fans, Hearts, & Folk Art, Jean Wells

Pattern Play, Doreen Speckmann

Picture This, Jean Wells and Marina Anderson

Pieced Clothing, Yvonne Porcella

Pieced Clothing Variations, Yvonne Porcella

PQME Series: Basket Quilt, Jean Wells

PQME Series: Bear's Paw Quilt, Jean Wells

PQME Series: Country Bunny Quilt, Jean Wells

PQME Series: Milky Way Quilt, Jean Wells

PQME Series: Nine-Patch Quilt, Jean Wells

PQME Series: Pinwheel Quilt, Jean Wells

PQME Series: Sawtooth Star Quilt, Jean Wells

PQME Series: Stars & Hearts Quilt, Jean Wells

Quilts, Quilts, and More Quilts! Diana McClun and Laura Nownes

Recollections, Judith Montano

Stitching Free: Easy Machine Pictures, Shirley Nilsson

Symmetry: A Design System for Quiltmakers, Ruth B. McDowell

3 Dimensional Design, Katie Pasquini

A Treasury of Quilt Labels, Susan McKelvey

Whimsical Animals, Miriam Gourley

For more information write for a free catalog from
C&T Publishing, P.O. Box 1456, Lafayette, CA 94549
(1-800-284-1114)